WORRIER TO WARRIOR
CONQUER ANXIETY & PANIC ATTACKS

Kate Ellis

Reviews

I feel so incredibly lucky to have found Kate! For several years I've had debilitating anxiety whenever I was traveling in a car. I felt like I would never be able to travel outside of my immediate neighborhood, I was at wits end. Then someone referred me to Kate! After just a couple of meetings with her I feel completely different. I actually took a ride, as a passenger, up a mountainous winding road. I truly never thought I would be able to do that. Thank you Kate, not just from me, my husband thanks you too! Marie schilder

I would highly recommend Kate to any of my family or friends. In one summer she was able to successfully correct patterns of anxiety that I have struggled with for years. She makes her clients her top priority and is available outside of scheduled sessions and regularly checks up on how you are doing. I have had a very positive experience with Kate and hope others keep an open mind about hypnotherapy and give it a try! Taylor Meyer

I had a great experience with Ms. Ellis, I came to see her after being recommended from a previous client about a few minor things I was noticing in myself that I wanted to improve. After the first session that included a cleansing, I felt relaxed and slept great for the proceeding few nights. Then, after two or three sessions I started to notice little positive changes in myself that were exactly why I came to see her. It was the best feeling to realize those little changes, but not only did I notice the changes, people would make comments about things they were noticing in me that reflected those same positive changes, it was quite empowering. I have recommended Ms. Kate Ellis to my friends, she does great, professional work. Emil Schaffroth

I went to Kate when I was at the end of, well at the end of myself. I was contemplating suicide and felt like a shell of a human being. I had battled extreme depression and eating disorders for over 15 years by the time I found Kate.

After I left our first session, I knew even though I had a long road ahead of me, that suicide was no longer a possibility. From there I continued to heal more and more with each session. After my initial program, I was a better version of myself than I had ever been. I had the strength in mind and spirit to propel myself into a new life. A new life where I felt true joy for the first time ever.

And that new life still has challenges!! Even years later, I continue to call Kate when I need a pep talk or even to do additional sessions when I need extra help and support overcoming things like my father's cancer diagnosis and eventual death. All along the journey, Kate has been a trusted guide and a loving friend.

I have sent many friends and family members to Kate. I recommend her to anyone looking to take back their life and move into a better version of themselves. I am deeply grateful for Kate being in my life. Kaycee Mitchell

Kate Ellis is very personable and has a true skill for helping others. She always makes you feel comfortable and safe. She is available to talk outside of the office from 10am-10pm for the well being of her clients. After the first session I had with her I felt calmer and in control of the anxiety. She has her own workbooks that she publishes to correspond with the therapy sessions. She is the only therapist that has helped me to a noticeable degree that family and friends noticed. I would recommend her to anyone! Larissa Lewis

Kate Ellis is a highly skilled, truly amazing person. She uses her gifts to empower and provide different views. She shares insight and wisdom in practical, life changing ways. I sought out Kate as part of a self-care plan. I left my first visit feeling optimistic, challenged and looking forward to my next visit. There is no doubt she is authentic and deeply cares. If you are reading reviews, searching, I have been there. Give Kate a call. She gets it. Ann Mclure

I have been blessed to know Kate Ellis for many years. She even did hypnotherapy classes at my store in Scottsdale Arizona. Kate is a amazingly gifted hypnotherapist! She has helped many people that I know to get better and to have their lives back in a very positive way. Her integrity is impeccable. Please make an appointment if you are ready to get help. Kates real passion and purpose is about the healing!!! Judith Manganiello

I'm very grateful to have been referred to Kate because she changed my life. I have been struggling with severe anxiety for several years and my fiancée referred me to Kate. I have never been under hypnosis or even considered it as a remedy for the anxiety, but after my consultation, I felt very confident in her abilities to be able to help me.

Every session I would feel a noticeable improvement until now I am now anxiety free. It doesn't happen overnight, but she was very clear about managing my expectations for results and each session was unique based on how I was reacting to the previous sessions. I only wish I had done this years ago because it's made a massive impact on my daily life. Justin Orsini

I began working with Kate over a decade ago. Finding someone that you can open up to with out judgment is rare. I initially began working with Kate for my anxiety and panic attacks. We quickly worked through my anxiety and moved into curing my migraines. She has helped me with insomnia, bouts of depression, public speaking and most recently with facilitating a natural birth. Kate is a true healer. I am forever grateful that our paths crossed. I will forever continue to recommend her for anyone looking to better any areas of their lives. Thank you Kate! Raquel Raney

Kate changed my life. She helped heal the one thing that Zoloft did for me, completely drug free and without anxiety attacks. She's great and I did 3 sessions. I my anxiety attacks went away after the first session. Then she took away more of my issues I struggled with the next two session. I'll be returning. I am a very satisfied client! Chelsea Hammond

I have an autoimmune illness that I endure chronic pain. Kate has helped me turn down the volume of the pain by hypnotherapy. I realized through our sessions that mental is just as an important component of managing your illness as medication is. Kate goes further than other therapists she understands where you are coming from and tackles the important issues. I have recommended her to my family and friends. I know first hand the changes she has helped me make. Elisa Brancati

Kate came into my life when I was at very low point, I was suffering from addiction and a severe depression. Her counseling and therapy changed my whole life. She set me on a path of healing and spiritual growth that help me to overcome the obstacles in my life. I am so grateful for her support and guidance through my troubled times. She is a person I know I can always count on to lift me up and give me hope. I can't thank her enough for the life she helped me win back. Thank so much kate for all that you do. Nate Ram

Kate changed not only my life but spirit and mended what was broken, everyday I wake up now ready for anything, any problem. I have no idea where I would be if she didn't come into my life thank you to this type of healing just isn't enough to give back she gave me access to never ending knowledge and guidance, she's unbelievable I couldn't be more grateful to have crossed paths with her. Like I said thank you just isn't enough for me to say to her for what she did for me. Anything can be possible when you want them to be. Robert Horhler

The Healing Quest Publishing
Scottsdale, Arizona

ISBN: 978-0-9898083-3-0

October 2014

Revision 2021

Printed in the United States of America.

Keys of Knowledge

☞ 99% of Anxiety & Panic attacks are rooted in projection into the future.

☞ In every moment you are either empowering of disempowering yourself.

☞ You are not your thoughts, you are the one who picks & chooses which to focus upon & thus empower.

☞ Your experiences of life are a direct result of your perception.

☞ Your perception is in part your foundational belief system.

☞ Your perception is in part a decision from experiences from your past.

☞ You are the creator and co-creator of your reality.

☞ You have no power or control over of what other people think or feel.

☞ The only power you have exists only in the present moment (the past is gone, the future is in process of being created).

☞ There are two emotions, joy and fear or sadness, all other expressions emerge from these.... Such as love, love is an expression of joy.

☞ Show me 10 minutes ago... show me 10 minutes from now, you can't... the only time that exists is the Present moment, where your power lives.

Contents

Section One

Section Two ~ Self-Hypnosis Scripts/Program

Section Three ~ Further

Section Four ~ Articles

Section Five

Section Six

Foreword

by C. Roy Hunter

Kate Ellis originally copyrighted *Worrier to Warrior* in 2014; but far more people need this important self-help book today than ever before — especially in light of the worldwide increases in stress and anxiety in 2020.

Many people suffer from fears, anxieties, agoraphobia, post-traumatic stress syndrome, obsessive/compulsive disorder, and/or other problems resulting from unresolved stress. How many people do you personally know who have one or more of these problems?

How many people do you know who are filled with resentment, shame, or guilt? ...or feel low self-worth without any apparent reason? They may also benefit from this book.

The author literally walks her talk, and shares her personal story with the readers. After successfully overcoming her fear of flying with hypnotherapy, she studied hypnosis seriously and made a career change. Walk with her as she walks the readers through her own journey of empowerment. She not only describes important concepts of the mind, she also tells you HOW you can overcome stress and anxiety.

Learn how to move from stress into your Comfort Zone, and re-direct negative feelings into energy that helps us move towards our goals, dreams, and aspirations.

Learn how to use your imagination to help create the reality you desire. It is YOUR imagination, and you can choose whatever you wish to imagine. When we imagine a bad outcome, that contributes to fears and anxiety. When we imagine a peaceful place, we can become more comfortable.

Additionally, we all have the ability to *choose* our thoughts. The greatest weapon against stress is our ability to choose one thought over another. Also, we can either react or *respond* when unexpected challenges appear. How can we do this? The pages of this book contain answers to the above.

We all have an innate ability to calm and center ourselves, which is a foundation of achieving our ideal self-empowerment. Kate provides important tips to help you — including (but not limited to) learning how to use self-hypnosis and benefit from it. Scripts are provided.

I first met Kate about 15 years ago, and she was already an experienced hypnotherapist. After becoming a published author myself years before the 21st Century, I have enjoyed the privilege of meeting several thousand hypnotherapists at numerous conferences and workshops. It would be impossible to remember all the professionals I meet; but Kate immediately impressed me with her strength of character and her passion for using hypnosis to help people.

Walk with her through the pages of her book — and may you become happier and more empowered!

--C. Roy Hunter

kae

Introduction

Worrier to Warrior, outlines anxiety and panic attacks, and other forms of anxiety such as OCD and PTSD. It also serves as a guide to obtain relief and remission, to correct anxiety and panic attacks. WTW is different from other books and programs available. It is a 'how to' or 'do it yourself' program that will enable you to understand what is occurring, insight to how the anxiety/panic attacks got started and ultimately, how to end the vicious cycle, which you may have found out only gets worse, manifesting as a panic attack and spiraling down into what is called an anxiety dis-order where your life becomes severely limited.

In over 30 years in private practice, I have created a protocol utilizing hypnotherapy and cognitive behavioral training, that corrects anxiety and panic attacks in three sessions. If you follow the program precisely, use the tools within, pay attention to all the specific details I point out, you will be completely successful and never have a full blown panic attack again, and manage anxieties as they occur over a life time. You will learn that it is your thinking that flips the "on" switch to the fight or flight or freeze response, which is your survival mechanism gone awry.

You do not need to agree with everything I say, philosophies. Such as I will state you are a mind, body, spirit... if you take exception to the word 'spirit', which is energy... change the word to; 'an electrical feedback system'.

Do pay close attention to words and language you are personally using, because they are either empowering you or disempowering you, period. I will ask you to be the mind or thought police for a period of time, to recognized how you are repeatedly programming yourself opposite of your desires and desired experiences in life, from solace to life success, or as the title implies; Worrier to Warrior.

Understand this clearly, you are not broken, it is simply a kink in your thinking process, and being YOU are the one choosing what thoughts to focus upon, you can change the thoughts that create the cycle of anxieties, and what is setting off the attacks.

You are an unending horizon, be prepared to change the rest of your life and how you experience it.

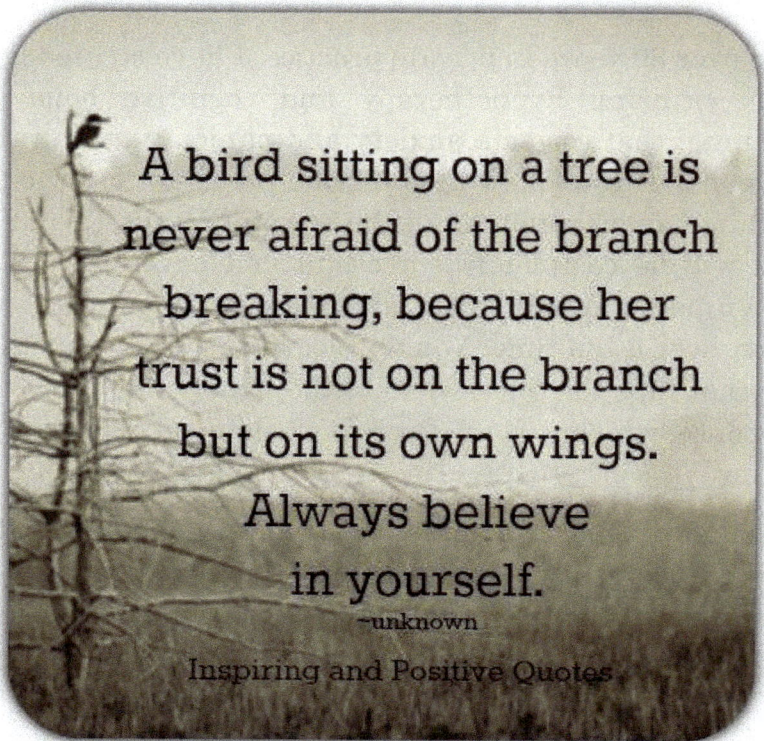

A bird sitting on a tree is never afraid of the branch breaking, because her trust is not on the branch but on its own wings. Always believe in yourself.
—unknown

Inspiring and Positive Quotes

Suggestion: Instead of saying or stating; "My anxiety" change it to "The anxiety" in your thoughts, in your speech.

The philosophy is 'owning' anxiety, like you own your shoes or car or refrigerator. Do you want to own anxiety?

Create a buffer between you and it, like a habit, does a habit 'own' you or is it just something you mindlessly practice? Time to become mindful.

Remember: Words convey Meaning and Intent.

> # We are continually either empowering or
>
> # disempowering ourselves by what we choose to focus upon.
>
> # Focus upon what you want, not what you do not want.
>
> # You are the creator of your personal reality. Period

"From the moment of my birth, the angels of anxiety, worry, and death stood at my side, followed me out when I played, followed me in the sun of springtime and in the glories of summer. They stood at my side in the evening when I closed my eyes, and intimidated me with death, hell, and eternal damnation. And I would often wake up at night and stare widely into the room: Am I in Hell?"

— Edvard Munch

I understand your journey

This is my personal journey with anxiety/panic and how by recognizing I was either empowering or disempowering myself with my very own thoughts, I liberated myself from struggle, fear and a nice rubber room.

My journey began with a troubled marriage and a sprint across Denver Stapleton Airport in the early 1980's. I had traveled to Arizona from Chicago to assist two women to begin new lives after having the courage to leave abusive relationships. I brought them to my Mom's house where they would be nurtured, where they could heal and begin anew without concern or worry their abusers could find them. I stayed in touch with my husband over the phone for the couple weeks I visited, having brought my daughter who was about 2 years old. During a particularly strained conversation the last words I heard from my husband was; "Bring my daughter back, but I don't care what happens to you." Deeply worried of what I would walk into back home, I hadn't slept three days before the flight. I felt strangely nervous, fidgety, I had no appetite and there was this buzzing, like white noise in my head and ears constantly.

The flight took off late, and I had to catch a connecting flight in Denver.   The pilot assured those transferring that a representative would meet and escort us all meeting the connecting flight at the gate. Well, that didn't happen. With toddler, suitcase, stroller in hand, weighing down my petite 104 lb frame, came last call for my connecting flight! I dashed along with other passengers across the airport, of course the terminal had to be at the opposite end. I just made it, having to bang on the plane door to let me in. I huffed and puffed, trying to catch my breath. We settled in and after we were in the air the stewardess asked if would care for anything to drink? I said; "yes, a cup of coffee would hit the spot." She smiled and brought it back. I took a sip, perhaps two and the white noise came back with a vengeance! My heart began to race, I began hyperventilating as though I was still running to catch the plane. Then I had the urgent need to go to the bathroom. The stewardess stopped by and seen I was sick and offered help. I asked her to please watch my child while I went to the restroom. I was in there nearly the entire flight with a sickness I had never experienced before.

My journey into anxiety and panic attacks begun. I had experienced them in the worst ways and over the next several years. It took a long time to even figure out what was wrong with me, all I knew is that my world became smaller and smaller as each attack took another piece of me, my ability to travel, enjoy a meal at a restaurant, taking an aspirin and eventually going to the grocery store.

After discovering what plagued me from a magazine article, which was in a large way a great relief, I set to get help for it. I was offered Valium from my doctor, but I was raising a family and couldn't be under the influence and be a parent. I sought counseling, but could not find a counselor who understood anxiety or panic. I did not have insurance that would cover treatment. Every place I sought help turned me away, primarily it resting on the almighty dollar, even catholic charities would not see me unless I had $95.00 up front, they wouldn't even work out a payment plan for me.

I launched into understanding the nature of personal reality and psychology and learned the mechanisms, triggers and solutions over time. I conquered it! Except for one last thing, traveling on an airplane. That is where it all began, and I couldn't get up the courage or risk a non-refundable ticket to try it out.

I attended a lecture at Daly College in Chicago where I lived, on Hypnosis. Ron Tater of the Hypnosis Foundation of Chicago spoke on hypnosis, hypnotherapy, how it can assist with phobia's, fears, etc... and, at the very end of the lecture he mentioned he trained people for hypnosis certification. This intrigued me. I decided to give it a try with my phobia of traveling on a plane. I made an appointment the very next day, had a consultation and then a singular hypnosis session and left with a recording of it. Not long afterwards, I sensed something shifted. When I thought of visiting my mother in Arizona, my stomach no longer seized, or felt that pang of fear. At this point, there was no way I was going to allow fear to lead my life. I booked a flight, packed the session tape, just in case, and boarded the flight. Yes, I was a bit apprehensive, but I conquered all the issues that previously caused panic and anxiety and knew I could do it. And I did! Once I corrected my thinking I had the world, my world by the tail, and the only limitations I have ever experienced from that point onward was the extent of my imagination.

I did indeed study hypnosis and related fields of medicine, psychology, counseling, anthropology, basically every 'ology' out there. I began a hypnotherapy practice and spent essentially the next 15 years learning.

I discovered a protocol of correcting anxiety/panic attacks in three sessions.

This holds true for nearly every client I have worked with. Our 'panic' button, which is called the fight/flight/freeze response is two hundred thousand years in the making. It protects us when we are mortally threatened, by either fighting the threat or running away from it. (and then some people freeze/hide) More often than not nowadays, the threat is not the loss of our lives, but our sense of control or feeling safe whether alone or with others. And it does not matter who you are, how smart, how old, if you are a male or female or a member of Mensa. Remember the Soprano's HBO series? Big strong Tony had a panic dis-order. Only he was treated with medications and talk therapy, which works in dealing with the symptoms, not however correcting the dis-order. And the dis-order is in the thought process. Your thoughts create. Take a moment to look around you. Everything you see was a thought in someone's mind until they made it a reality.

How powerful, a thought.

You are a most powerful person, and if you are suffering with anxiety or panic, know there is relief, remission and corrected with a specialist. Not every counselor or hypnotherapist specializes, just like not every doctor is familiar with every nuance of medicine. Ask the professional who you are seeing if they are successful in <u>correcting</u> anxiety/ panic attacks, and do not be surprised it may take a few interviews before you find the perfect fit.

Let me assure you, anxiety and panic attacks are not a life sentence. You can correct it permanently and never deal with it again and discover what opportunity it has for you. To be a stronger person? To realize how powerful you are that a thought, a simple thought can create this kind of havoc in your life? You are an unending horizon.

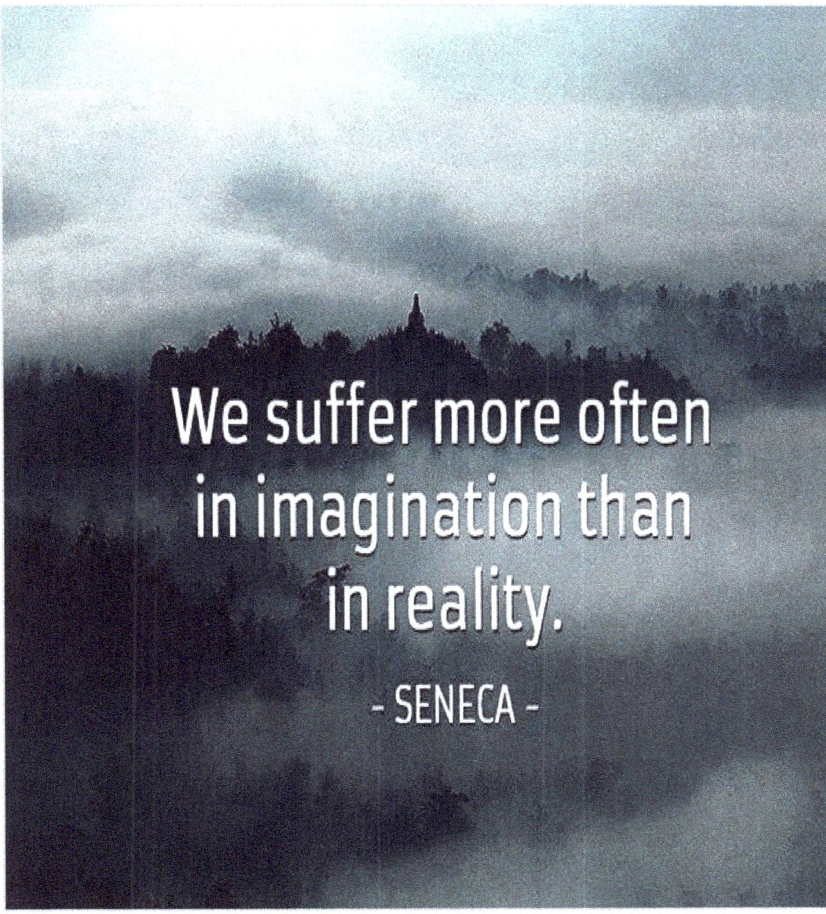
We suffer more often
in imagination than
in reality.
- SENECA -

mind.

noun. a beautiful servant,
a dangerous master.

OSHO

Anxiety/Panic Checklist

An anxiety/panic attack affects your mind, your body, and your behavior. During an attack, you become worried and anxious about something you believe will be danger-ous in the future. Then your mind and body become fo-cused on this fear. You may have physical sensations such as tension, shakiness, stomach distress, or sweating. Fo-cusing on these concerns, you may prepare yourself either by avoiding certain places and activities, by constantly checking to make sure you are safe, or by procrastinating because your excess worry is blocking concentration.

Here is a checklist of anxiety symptoms:

PHYSIOLOGICAL RESPONSE

☐ Dry Mouth

☐ Tightness in Chest

☐ Butterflies in Stomach

☐ Hot/Cold Flashes

☐ Rapid, Pounding Heartbeat

☐ Weakness All Over

☐ Hyperventilation

☐ Sweaty All Over
☐ Blurred Vision
☐ Pressure in head
☐ Rubbery legs/shaking

☐ Racing Thoughts

☐ Heart Palpitations

☐ Dizziness

☐ Fatigue

☐ Tremors/Shakiness

☐ Confusion

☐ Muscle Tension/
   Aches

☐ Tingling or Numbness
   in hands/feet
☐ Shortness of Breath

COGNITIVE RESPONSES

- I can't Breath
- I'm having a Heart Attack
- I'm going Crazy
- I am Dying
- I'm Trapped
- I could Faint
- People are Looking at me

- I can't do it
- I gotta get out of here
- I can't go out
- I'll make a fool of myself
- I can't go alone
- I might Vomit
- I might lose Control

EMOTIONAL RESPONSES

- Fear
- Panic
- Uneasy
- Trapped, no way out
- Loss of control
- Criticized
- Angry

- Keyed up/on edge
- Excessive worry
- Feelings of doom/gloom
- Isolated or lonely
- Embarrassed
- Rejected
- Depressed

Avoiding Crowds/Stores/Social Gatherings/Driving
Malls, Meetings/Restaurants/Long Lines/Traveling Alone

If you checked three or more ask yourself:

1) Is fear of an anxiety attack limiting my involvement in life?

2) Am I avoiding everyday situations?

3) Do I worry and feel tense most of the time?

4) Do I want to take medications that only manage symp-toms, or be done with this once and for all time?

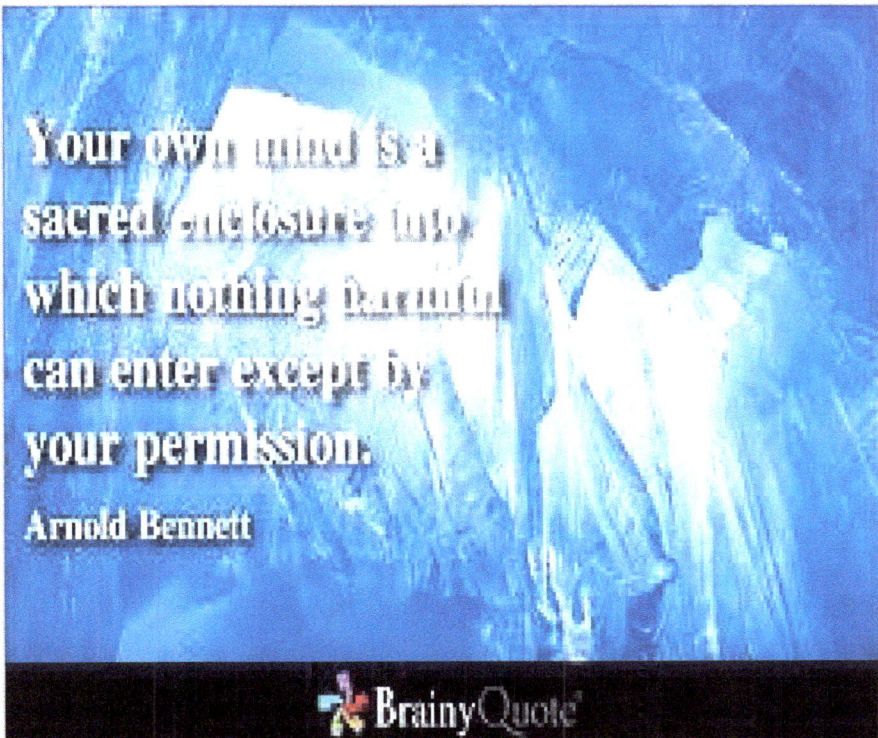

Your own mind is a sacred enclosure into which nothing harmful can enter except by your permission.

Arnold Bennett

BrainyQuote

Five basic truths:

1. Everything changes.
2. Things don't go like you plan.
3. Life's not fair.
4. There's going to be pain...

   (suffering is optional)
5. People won't always be loving or loyal.

Embrace these facts and you will liberate yourself from struggle.

Varying Levels/Expressions of
Anxiety Dis-Orders

Sometimes the physical symptoms of anxiety and anxiety/panic attacks send sufferers to emergency rooms and doctors offices in an attempt to uncover an underlying medical illness. Most often people, more often than not, women, are told that there is nothing physically wrong.

Many people with anxiety dis-order experience shortness of breath or sensations that they are smothering. These symptoms are often described as feeling like not being able to get enough air into the lungs. Since we need to breathe to sustain life, these symptoms quickly bring about a sense of panic and fear. If you feel like you can't catch your breath or are smothering, it may seem logical to conclude that you may faint, or even die, from lack of oxygen. But in reality, these sensations are not life threatening or dangerous and people rarely faint, to their chagrin.

You may experience frequent muscle tension. In fact, chronic muscle tension may be so automatic that it seems normal, and you may have forgotten what it feels like when your muscles are completely relaxed, especially in the jaw, clenching your teeth, the neck, upper back and shoulders.

About 50% to 66% of women and 35% to 40% of men who have an anxiety dis-order suffer from frequent headaches. And, people with anxiety dis-order are up to seven times more likely to suffer the most severe of all headaches -- migraine. One study showed that two out of three patients with panic dis-order met the criteria for problem headaches, with migraine being the most prevalent form.

Gastrointestinal disturbances commonly include symp-toms of stomach pain, heartburn, diarrhea, constipation, nausea, vomiting, spastic bowel/irritable, Crohns dis-ease.

About 40% of people with anxiety dis-order experience pain in their chest. The first thought is that you are ex-periencing a possible heart attack or an other cardiac event. This possibility sends many people to the nearest emergency room for help. But, often chest pain associated with anxiety dis-order is not related to the heart and is not, generally, considered serious.

About one-third of people who have an anxiety dis-order will develop a condition called agoraphobia. The main symptom of agoraphobia is intense fear, a panic response of being in certain situations often in public in which es-cape is difficult or potentially embarrassing, or where help is not readily available. More specifically, the focus is on the fear of having a anxiety attack in such situations.

The fear associated with agoraphobia is so intense that the person will usually go to great lengths to avoid the feared situations. Common situations that bring about a panic response due to agoraphobia include leaving home alone, staying home alone, traveling by car, train, plane or bus, being in an elevator, being in a crowd, being in a large store or mall, being in a confined area, being on a bridge or standing in a line.

Once the symptoms of an anxiety dis-order begin, agora-phobia can take a little time to develop, or it can come on rather quickly. Some sufferers believe their agoraphobic symptoms began after their first anxiety/panic attack.

Once agoraphobia takes root, avoidance behaviors often multiply quickly, and daily life becomes defined by a "comfort zone." The comfort zone includes the places, people, situations or events that bring about the least amount of anxiety. Going outside of the comfort zone is extremely difficult, distressing, if not impossible.

How agoraphobia accelerates:

Imagine you're driving on a highway and without warning you experience a dreaded sense of doom. Your heart begins to race wildly; your hands are shaking as you try to grip the steering wheel. It seems difficult to get air into your lungs, and you feel dizzy. There is no place to pull over, and you are completely at the mercy of this horrific thing that is happening. You wonder if you might be having a heart attack or dying from some strange, unknown illness. As you are able to exit on an off ramp, you begin to calm down. You are still shaken, but you are regaining some composure.

You start thinking on what could have happened if you had lost consciousness or were unable to maintain control of your car when you were driving on the highway. You think; "What if I got into a car accident? What if I had to stop my car abruptly in traffic and people started blowing their horns and yelling at me?" The logical answer to maintain your safety and escape potential embarrassment seems to be to avoid that highway... or maybe, all highways.

But, then it happens again... this time while you're standing in line at a grocery store. You've just emptied your cart onto the conveyor belt and the panic hits you. Your heart is racing, you're sweating, and you can't seem to get enough air or you are hyperventilating. You imagine that you may collapse right there, or you think about the embarrassment of losing control, and visualize yourself screaming and running out of the store. Somehow you manage to stand there while the clerk completes ringing up your purchase. When you exit the store, your legs are weak and your hands are shaking, but you feel a sense of relief. You now start to avoid long grocery store lines, or maybe, waiting in any lines.

Your comfort zone continues to be defined by these experiences. You may begin to drive only on roads with an emergency pull-off shoulder. Maybe you just shop at small convenience stores with less people and an exit that's always nearby. Or, perhaps you only venture out when you are with someone who will be able to help you in case you start to panic again. In a worst case scenario, you don't leave your home at all.

Addressing the issue:

The symptoms of agoraphobia can be frightening and potentially disabling. But, the majority of sufferers find significant relief with corrective treatment. The sooner corrective treatment begins after the onset of agoraphobia, the more quickly symptom reduction or elimination will be realized. However, even those with long-term symptoms will experience improvement with treatment, and most will regain the freedom to resume many of the activities you once enjoyed.

Anxiety dis-order occurs with or without agoraphobia, or the fear of panic-induced situations in which escape would be difficult or embarrassing.

Similar Conditions to Anxiety Dis-order:

It is not uncommon for those with anxiety dis-order to experience co-occurring anxiety-related or mood disorders, such as depression or social anxiety, OCD (Obsessive/Compulsive), PTS&D (Post Traumatic Stress)

People with social anxiety dis-order have an irrational fear of being watched, judged or evaluated, or of embarrassing or humiliating themselves. The anxiety and discomfort becomes so extreme that it interferes with daily functioning. Social anxiety is one of the most common anxiety issues with up to 13% of the general population experiencing symptoms at some point in their life.

The difference between normal shyness and social anxiety relates to the severity and persistence of the symptoms that are experienced, both emotional and physical symptoms.

Some of the emotional symptoms include:

- intense fear of situations where you don't know other people
- fear of situations where you will be judged
- anxiety about being embarrassed or humiliated
- fear that others will notice your anxiety
- fear and dread of upcoming events weeks in advance

Examples of physical symptoms include:

- blushing
- profuse sweating
- trembling hands
- muscle tension
- racing heart
- rubbery legs

The anxiety may be specific to one type of social or performance; such as addressing a group or colleagues in a meeting at work, or it may be in all situations dealing with people or crowds. Some of the situations that are common triggers include interacting with strangers, making eye contact, or initiating conversations. Public speaking and social anxiety are the top most commonly experienced.

Several factors often occurs in development these issues. These include but are not limited to:

- having an overly critical, controlling or protective parent
- being bullied or teased as a child
- family conflict or sexual abuse
- a shy, timid or withdrawn temperament as a child
- or a trauma

One of the clients mentioned in this book who had panic attacks as a child was traumatized by his elder brothers, being the youngest of three boys. They would routinely gang up on him and lock him in closets, under couches, to this day he is claustrophobic.

Obsessive/Compulsive Dis-order, or OCD is an anxiety dis-order on steroids as I call it. Question: Does the number 'six' cause any feelings of discomfort?

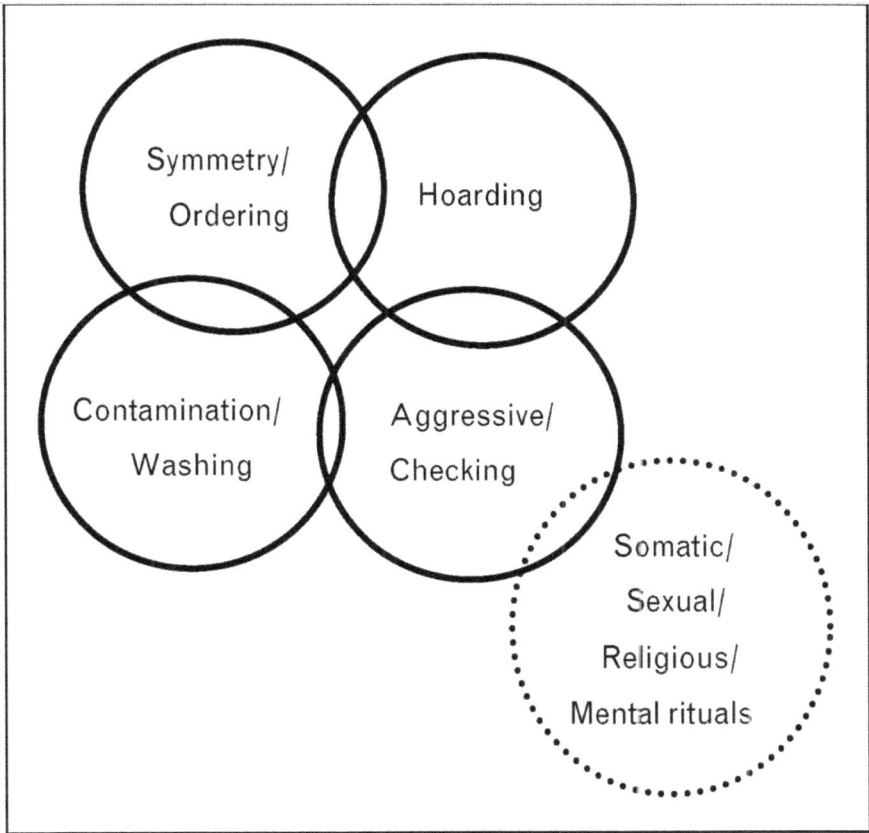

Most studies consistently identified four symptom dimensions. Some studies identified a fifth dimension consisting (in various combinations) of somatic, sexual, religious obsessions and mental rituals ('pure obsessions') but more research is needed to determine its validity. In most studies these pure obsessions were highly correlated with checking symptoms and loaded on a single factor named obsessions/checking. Note the overlap between these dimensions as mono-symptomatic patients are very rare.

Table 1. Common Obsessions and Compulsions

Obsessions

- Aggressive impulses (e.g., hurting a child or parent)
- Contamination (e.g., becoming contaminated by shaking hands with someone)
- Need for order (e.g., extreme distress when objects are asymmetrical or out of order)
- Religion (e.g., blasphemous thoughts or worry about unknowingly sinning)
- Repeated doubts (e.g., wondering whether a door was left unlocked)
- Sexual imagery (e.g., recurrent pornographic images)

Compulsions

- Checking (e.g., repeatedly checking appliances, alarms, or locks)
- Cleaning (e.g., repetitive handwashing)
- Hoarding (e.g., saving useless items or trash)
- Mental acts (e.g., counting, praying, or silently repeating words)
- Ordering (e.g., rearranging objects to achieve symmetry)
- Reassurance-seeking (e.g., repetitively asking others for reassurance)
- Repetitive actions (e.g., repeatedly walking in and out of a doorway)

Source: Reference 1.

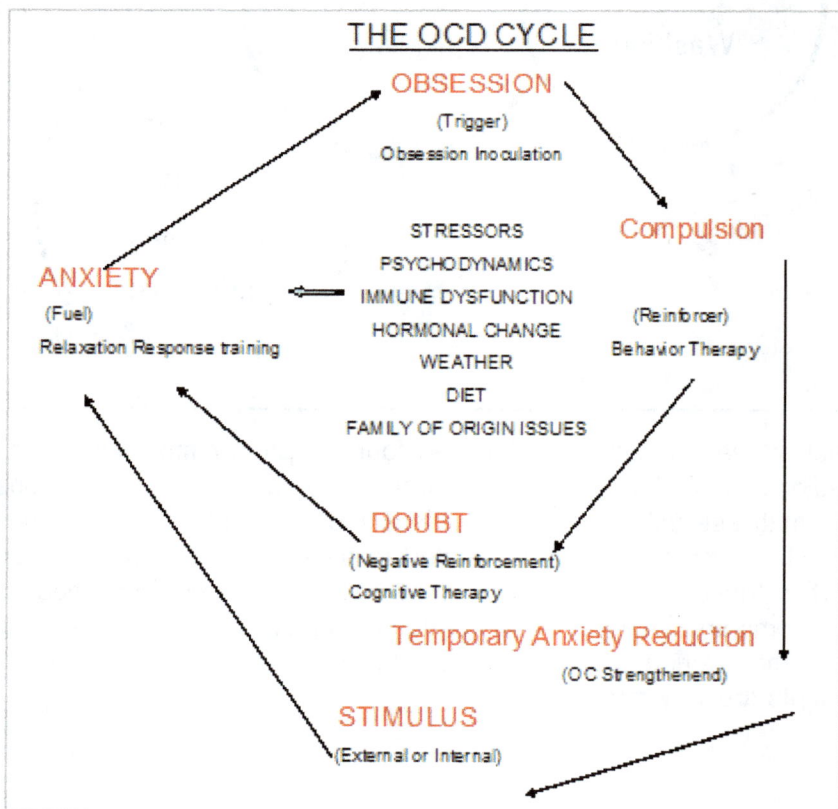

THE OCD CYCLE

OBSESSION
(Trigger)
Obsession Inoculation

STRESSORS
PSYCHODYNAMICS
IMMUNE DYSFUNCTION
HORMONAL CHANGE
WEATHER
DIET
FAMILY OF ORIGIN ISSUES

Compulsion
(Reinforcer)
Behavior Therapy

ANXIETY
(Fuel)
Relaxation Response training

DOUBT
(Negative Reinforcement)
Cognitive Therapy

Temporary Anxiety Reduction
(OC Strengthenend)

STIMULUS
(External or Internal)

The 4 phases of Cognitive Therapy for OCD

Phase	Description
Relabel	First of all the individual should tell himself that his hands are not dirty, even though he may feel that they are dirty.
Reattribute	The individual is told to give a message to his brain that "the chemical in his brain s imbalance and therefore his brain is giving him wrong messages." For example, the person may tell himself this: "It is the OCD that is causing me to feel this way. My hands are not dirty and nothing is wrong with them."
Refocus	The individual is told to divert his attention. For example, when an OCD though comes up, he quickly indulges himself in some other behaviours.
Revalue	The individual is told not to give importance to his OCD thoughts. For example, when an OCD thought comes up, he tells himself that "This is just my stupid obsession. There is no need to pay any attention to it."

Utilizing Hypnotherapy with Cognitive behavior techniques greatly accelerates and enhances one's ability to cope or release the anxiety associated with shifting perceptions. What keeps you stuck in a behavior are the uncomfortable feelings that arise with what seems like a vengeance. The core issues lie within the subconscious, so the combination of both therapeutic approaches, CBT & Hypnotherapy greatly increase your ability to shift the symptoms, alarm signals going off in your mind, giving you back control of your choice of how you are going to perceive a threat, whether real or imaginary/fear based.

As you can see on the graphic on the following page, Post Traumatic Stress is a spiraling event and is a spirit killer. PTS is not only something soldiers experience, it can be any trauma as illustrated in the graphs.

12 Steps of PTSD

Randy J. Hartman, Ph.D

Acute Anxiety	Panic/anxiety episodes
Depression	Self-esteem in a downward spiral
Resentment	Distrusting others
Anger	Fight or flight developing
Fear	PTSD is now forming
Anxiety	Mixed episodes occur
Self-Worth Dissipating	Feeling worthless
Shame	Filled with shame; who else knows?
Guilt	Feeling guilty; how responsible am I?
Confusion	Trying to remember; can I trust my memory?
Pain	Emotional, spiritual & physical pain
Activating Event(s)	Any event that causes distress

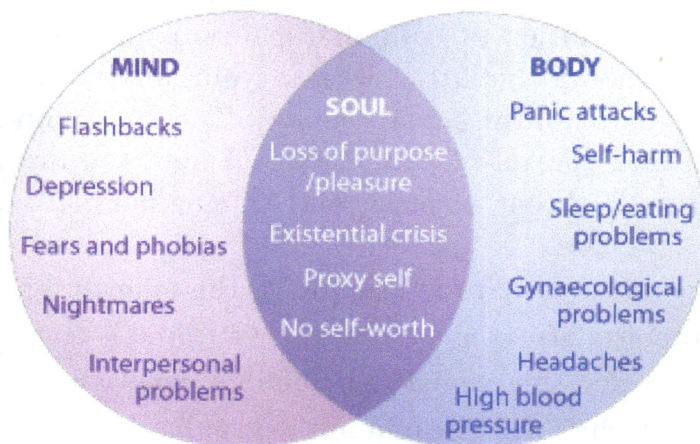

MIND

Flashbacks

Depression

Fears and phobias

Nightmares

Interpersonal problems

SOUL

Loss of purpose /pleasure

Existential crisis

Proxy self

No self-worth

BODY

Panic attacks

Self-harm

Sleep/eating problems

Gynaecological problems

Headaches

High blood pressure

I had a client who was driving home during rush hour. As she reached the middle of an intersection, a driver in the opposite direction made a left in front of her, hitting the vehicle and sending it careening across the road into a light pole on the corner, where three young boys near the age of 10 where waiting to cross the street. The car just missed the boys, thankfully. She received some debilitating injuries that required surgery and time to heal, but not life threatening. What was most difficult for her to get over was the thought of; "What if I hit those children." It haunted her every day. With many PTS sufferers, it is that one question. 'what if' that spins one out of control, and the lack of control in a situation as described that continues the paralyzing thoughts, feelings, motion of emotions, and the subconscious' ability to bring recall in absolute detail, a past event.

I have found people who are dealing with PTS are deeply compassionate, caring persons, and assume 100% responsibility.

> **Everyone makes mistakes in life, but that doesn't mean they have to pay for them the rest of their life.**
> **sometimes good people make bad choices, It doesn't mean they are bad.**
> **It means they are human.**

STRENGTH DOESN'T COME FROM WHAT YOU **CAN** DO. IT COMES FROM **OVERCOMING** THE THINGS YOU ONCE THOUGHT YOU **COULDN'T**.

You will notice I hyphenate "disorder."

(dis-order)

Language is crucial by inadvertently giving your subconscious mind an instruction to react as though a true threat is occurring. If you take the word apart, "dis" actually means "apart." "Order" means arrangement, organization, structure, system.

When a doctor or perceived authority figure states you have a "disorder", you tend to believe there is something seriously wrong with you.

Actually, it is a dis-order in your thinking. Like tidying a room, item by item eventually order and comfort is achieved.

Don't be surprised if this is 'familiar'

Did you know that anxiety dis-orders tends to run in families? It is only in the last 10-20 years that 'anxiety dis-order' has been labeled as such. In many cases it was called a nervous breakdown.

People tend to self medicate, such as drinking alcohol, often not realizing they are doing so. It is expressed in a variety of ways, one relative may have phobias while another may be an alcoholic or drug abuser. Other expressions can be being a perfectionist, or lazy, while others may have untoward clutter or even hording to the other extreme of a magazine perfect house, staying in a negative or even abusive relationship, eating/body issues.

There is most certainly a genetic component, but that does not mean you are doomed for life. Anxiety issues are behavioral at it's core, and thus can be corrected, adjusted or managed.

One of the most fascinating thing I have found with anxiety/panic attacks is they have an intriguing pattern. When one experiences a panic attack out of the blue, it tends more often than not to be approximately 2 1/2 years after a trauma. The death of a loved one, loss of a job or relationship. Something that rocked your world. Then one day you are in the grocery store reaching for a box of cereal and you begin to profusely sweat, hands begin shaking, your heart races, your thoughts are bouncing around your head like a hundred stinging bees, you feel as though you may faint or run screaming, embarrassing yourself. Your only focus is to get out of there! You get to your car, or someplace where you feel safe and begin to calm down. I have found this pattern over and over again, with 99% of my clients experiencing their first anxiety/ panic attack. The problem begins when you begin to fear having another one.

I call it, "the fear of the fear of the fear."

You fear having another one so you begin to avoid situations which may create one. If the anxiety issue is not nipped in the bud, it can spiral so out of control that your world becomes smaller and smaller.

Most people will have one or two anxiety/panic attacks in their lifetime, and that is the end of it. But if the core issues are not addressed, which is at it's root; feeling <u>safe in this world</u>, in <u>control in and of your life</u> it becomes a way of life, a very painful life. Fear, doubt, dread begins to erode self-confidence, self-esteem, self-worth. It is a downward spiral. The interest in writing this book is not to get into the nitty gritty of deep psychological materials. The intention is to help you have a basic understanding of what you are dealing with, and how to eradicate it from your life.

Who experiences anxiety or panic attacks; anyone from anywhere. From every socioeconomic background, any race, religion, any woman, man or child. No one is impervious because it's roots are your survival instincts, the fight/flight/freeze response, which is out of whack. Technically it is a mental dis-order, but really, if there was a truer label, it is a Thinking Dis-order. Do not be afraid of things labeled as 'disorders'. In order for your doctor or healthcare provider to treat what ails you, there needs to be what is called medical billing code, it is a number that designates a diagnosis which then allows insurance companies to be charged for your appointment and possible medications. Perhaps you have heard recently of doctors wanting to call obesity a 'disorder'. If the FDA approves the label, then insurance companies can be charged for all sorts of weight loss approaches, diets, medications, surgeries, you name it. Money, that is the bottom line.

Speaking of doctors, whether mental or medical, most unfortunately do not realize there is a corrective treatment for anxiety/panic attack issues. They do their best to help you by prescribing a medication they feel will help your symptoms, but that is all they treat, the symptoms. If you are really unlucky, you will be prescribed an antidepressant. Recently I have soft launched an educational initiative on the correction of anxiety dis-orders, to bring education and awareness that there are professionals out there who specifically deal with it; specialists. Not even a lot of psychologists are aware, so do not hate your healthcare provider. It is only the last 20-30 years where your primary caregiver refers you to a specialist, such as a podiatrist for foot issues, or a cardiologist for heart issues. Not all psychologists 'specialize' in anxiety issues, specifically, correction.

It is your perception that triggers the fight/flight/freeze response. What is 'perception'? It is what you believe about something, it is your truth (at the moment). This was discussed in the previous pages regarding the 'comfort zone'.

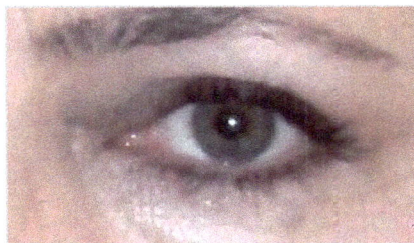

Be grateful for
all the obstacles
in your life.
They have
strengthened you as
you continue with
your journey.

mediawebagor.com

For loved ones & friends

Note to Family, Friend, Loved one's: Anxiety/panic attacks are a survival instinct reaction, your loved one is not exaggerating their fear. They are truly incapable of coping with certain situations.

It can be easy after a while to become frustrated, especially if you have placed or become, more often than not unknowingly, as their support system. Picking up the slack in life if they cannot get out of the house, or freak out when you arrive at a destination only to have to turn around and go back home. Home, one of the only places they feel a sense of safety.

Believe it or not, if your loved one has a social anxiety or agoraphobia, and they agreed to go out, this has been a monumental task, especially if they actually got out of the house, into the car. Depending on how long the plans were in place, know that they have been in extreme emotional turmoil from the word go.

Our survival instincts are powerful, as you are now quite aware. Imagine this: You are crossing a high traffic busy street during rush hour. There are loud noises all around you, horns beeping, cars whooshing, brakes screeching, people talking though you cannot make out exactly what they are saying, like white noise all around you. You are attempting to cross this busy street with hundreds of vehicles all around you, but you cross at a safe place, a crosswalk obeying the signal.

The light changes from red to green, you step off the curb and two or three steps in you become stuck in quick set cement up to your knees. You cannot move, you are hopelessly stuck, and the indicator with the orange hand comes on blinking... you know the light is about to change.

Now the main traffic has stopped and the left turn traffic is heavy, moving through the turn arrow... and you, stuck there in the middle of the street is obstructed from view of the soon on-coming traffic. You are aware of all of these things. You furiously work to extricate yourself but you can't.

You are now freaking out, you may be praying with fervor, the traffic and noise is so loud you know that if you scream no one will hear you, and now the traffic signal has changed and you see a large truck heading towards you... slow at first, but unrelenting. You may be waving your arms wildly and yelling to attract attention, but no one can see you or hear you and you KNOW you are going to die. Your fear of death is in your face and there is nothing you can do to change it.

This is an insight as to what your loved one or friend is experiencing every time an anxiety/panic attack occurs. Mortal threat.

Think now about how long it would take you to calm down after such a harrowing incident?

Somehow, at the very last moment the truck driver sees you and slams on the brakes and stops two inches from your face. You can smell the diesel fuel in your nostrils, the heat of the engine on your body, sweat is pouring off of your body as you are uncontrollably trembling. Your heart is beating so hard you feel as though it is going to explode inside your chest or have a heart attack. You are still stuck in the cement, and people are now all around you, doing their level best to help you. You are so upset you may throw up, you fear you may soil yourself, there is a ringing in your ears that is deafening. You are hyperventilating but at the same time cannot seem to catch your breath.

Eventually you are released and make your way home, the only place you want to be, you forget anything else, where you were going or who you were to meet. The experience is so horrific there is only one place that you know is safe, home.

Now, safe inside your home you work at calming down, but over and over the experience you just had keeps going on and on in your mind. After a while, you are able to distract yourself by watching TV or calling a friend and telling them what just happened, and by chatting you begin to calm down, because you called a friend or loved one, a safe person. You may even grab a glass of wine, beer or spirits to further calm yourself... and it works.

Or your family comes home and you lay in your hunny's arms and begin to calm down, again, feeling safe, in control.

These specific examples of alcohol or a specific person is intentional. People who suffer with anxiety/panic attacks will at some point discover a substance or person allows them to feel safe. However, this can be a treacherous road, where they can begin abusing substances or become clingy/needy, requiring you to help them in situations they feel the same level of threat as described in the scenario.

This is especially true of people with OCD. You become an extension of their sense of safety, control in and of their life and ability to function. This is a very slippery slope, here is an example:

I had a client with OCD (obsessive/compulsive disorder). She had a germ phobia (Mysophobia) that was pretty extensive and debilitating. When she would freak out, her husband did everything he could to comfort her, being pulled further and further into her mania. Not only did she obsess constantly, washing her hands and surfaces around the house, she required the family members to follow suit as well, and if they did not, she would have a panic attack, appearing to be hysterical, and the family members found it easier to just acquiesce and do as she demanded.

It is a slippery slope because now her behavior is being enabled, which allowed her to continue to descend into her germ phobia, controlling every single individuals actions in the house. If someone, such as the mailman knocked on the door, and it was opened, immediately afterward she demanded (through her panic) the house needed to be thoroughly cleaned. This entailed the walls, drapes, all surfaces, carpets, clothes they were wearing at the time, etc. Nothing could be brought into the house without it being as sterilized as possible, or scrubbed with bleach. Every single grocery, everything.

When entering the house, family members had to remove their clothes and placed in the laundry and thoroughly shower. When the step-daughter visited, she was actually required to disrobe outside the front door, be carried on her fathers back (she was 14) through the house directly into the shower.

She pulled everyone into her nightmare. When we love someone, we can unknowingly be sucked into their world, attempting to help them or avoid the hours of anxiety and panic they feel, and you go through as well as an outsider looking in.

There are ways you can help them without playing into their fears and panic. Remind them they are safe. Remind them to breathe slowly and deeply, gaining control of their autonomic nervous system. Give them room temperature water and have them sip it slowly to leach the excess adrenaline coursing through their body that is producing the physiological symptoms, which are frightening. Sometimes changing the location is a good thing, taking a walk outside or around the house. A cup of mint tea or a spearmint breath mint will also calm the symptoms. Remind them that again they are safe and it is only a thought and the feelings will pass shortly.

Depending on the severity of their anxiety/panic attack, sometimes leaving them alone for a little while so they can calm themselves. In this case, give them a time line of when you will return, such as 45 minutes or an hour or fifteen minutes... give them enough space to relax and calm themselves, but let them know you will return.

If they are dealing with OCD, do your level best not to play into their fears, and go through the steps listed above. If you acquiesce to their phobia, and wash your hands or whatever ritual they need you to do, it will not help them but continue to enable the behavior. After they are calm, at a different time, perhaps the following day, look for a specialist, perhaps a list of several and have a chit chat, give them the list and let them know they need assistance to correct the anxiety, panic or phobia.

I designed this chapter specifically for loved ones and friends of those who suffer with anxiety/panic attacks. Understand that not every counselor or therapist specializes in anxiety dis-orders. Sometimes to begin with a Primary Care Physician is the place to start. If medication is suggested, make it nothing at first but valium or zanax, or from the health food store, Calms, valerian, chamomile or even Samee. Avoid antidepressants or psychotropic medications... first of all, antidepressants if effective, will only suppress symptoms, not correct them. Secondly, when they do go for treatment or correction, it will take a longer time to get them off these types of medications that change brain chemistry and has unpleasant side effects.

There are a small segment of people who need medications, a majority do not, they need an expert/specialist. Anxiety/panic dis-order is not a disease such as a heart condition or diabetes in which needs to be constantly monitored. It is a thinking dis-order at its essential level, and need to be taught what is going on and that they can gain not only control, but ultimately correction. Medication is a bridge to stabilize until the right therapist is found.

Think of it like this; you broke your arm bone. You see a doctor and they refer you to a specialist, an orthopedist. You have an exam and consultation, it is determined you do not need surgery but the bone set and placed in a cast until the body heals. Once the cast is removed, you will never break your arm in the same place ever again, as a matter of fact, the healed fracture is stronger than the bone on either side. It is very similar to an anxiety/panic dis-order, once it is corrected, your loved one will never have a full blown panic attack again, their fight/flight/freeze response 'button' has been re-set back to normal... up to now it was stuck in the on position, so any slight threat throws the symptoms into high gear. I am specifying anxiety/panic attacks. This does not take long at all to correct, most people require three sessions, and results will occur with the first. Keep this in mind when consulting with a counselor. Additionally, a counseling hypnotherapist is the specific specialist required, however, EFT, (emotional freedom technique) is also known to correct with the right practitioner, it is also referred to as Tapping or NLP (Neural linguistic programming).

It takes a combination of cognitive behavior techniques and hypnotherapy found to correct at both the conscious and subconscious levels of mind activity. Some people with more intense issue require more time to correct, such as ODC, 12-24 session is normal, if the family members are cooperative that is, because now it is a family issue in which needs to adjust their behavior and remind their loved one calming techniques, etc.

Even though your friend or loved one can gain control and correct anxiety/panic attacks, please do not mistake this as it being something they are using to manipulate you, more often than not, it is out of their control until they learn new skills and conquer their very real fears. Often a trauma occurred a couple years previous to on-set, then out of the blue they are hit with these debilitating physiological symptoms and downward emotional spiral.

Every human being is susceptible to anxiety/panic attacks, remember, it is our survival mechanism gone out of whack. No matter who you are, where you come from, man, woman, child, socioeconomic status, intellect, race... if you are sentient, you have a survival mechanism and it can be wicked fierce. Negative, repetitive thinking prevents the release of essential balances of brain chemicals, hormones.

Forgiveness is a transcendent force that re-leases you from far more than the individual with whom you have a painful history. Forgiveness releases you from the ego state of consciousness that clings to a need for justice built around the fear of being humiliated, based on our prior experiences of humiliation. Forgiveness is essential to healing, because it requires you to surrender your ego's need to have a life fall into place around your personal version of justice. Caroline Myss

... And what Caroline states is true, including yourself, most importantly yourself. Consider yourself a Being in a constant state of becoming, evolving, growing and learning. We do not learn by being right, we learn through our errors. It is okay to be wrong. There is no such thing as 'perfect', it is a concept.

If I walk outside and it is a beautiful sun shiny day and I say it is perfect, then the following day I walk out and it is a sun shiny day and say it is perfect, am I lying?

Perception (from the Latin *perceptio, percipio*) is the organization, identification, and interpretation of sensory information in order to represent and understand of the environment.

All perception involves signals in the nervous system which in turn result from physical or chemical stimulation of the sense organs. For example, vision involves light striking the retina of the eye, smell is mediated by odor molecules and hearing involves pressure waves.

Perception is not the passive receipt of these signals, but is shaped by learning, memory, expectation and attention.

Perception involves these "top-down" effects as well as the "bottom-up" process of processing sensory input. The "bottom-up" processing transforms low-level information to higher-level information (e.g., extracts shapes for object recognition). The "top-down" processing refers to a person's concept and expectations (knowledge), and selective mechanisms (attention) that influence perception.

Perception depends on complex functions of the nervous system, but subjectively seems mostly effortless because this processing happens outside conscious awareness.

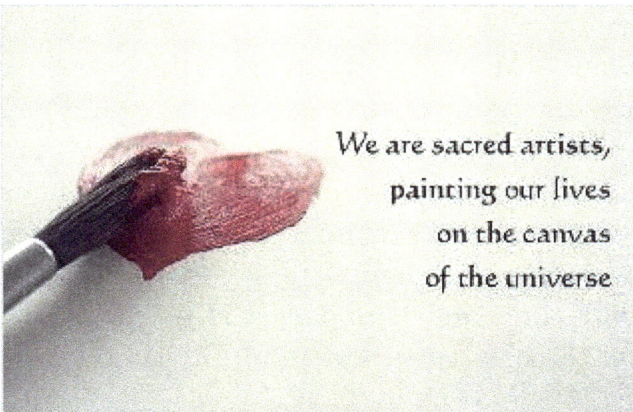

We are sacred artists,
painting our lives
on the canvas
of the universe

How Effective Is Hypnosis?

Results of Comparative Study
by *American Health Magazine:*

Psychoanalysis:
38% recovery after 600 sessions

Behavior Therapy:
72% recovery after 22 sessions

Hypnotherapy:
93% recovery after 6 sessions

Utilizing the combination of cognitive behavior training and hypnotherapy cuts the sessions down to three for 99% of my clients. Meaning; the panic attacks are corrected, essentially the panic button reset to neutral. For some clients who have a deep habituation of anxiety, such as issues with self trust, fear of change, self esteem or self worth issues can take more sessions. Learning to take your power back, the ability to say 'no' when you need to honor your time and boundaries is a process. However take note, the panic attacks are totally gone.

What is Hypnosis

There is nothing mysterious about hypnosis, it is essentially the shifting of attention or perception. You do this many times throughout your day. Such as when you sit down to write a list of things to do or a grocery list, you are shifting your ego (outward oriented) attention to an inner attention. Such as remembering and thinking about what you are writing.

The ego is a level of mind activity geared toward reacting/responding to the outside world.

The subconscious is a level of mind activity that allows you to smoothly operate in the world.

What do I mean by that... Your subconscious mind is your success mechanism, anytime you want to drive your car, each time you enter the vehicle you do not need to *remember* how to drive the car, you simply stick the key in the ignition and go. Or brushing your teeth, you do not need to *remember* which hand grabs the toothpaste and which hand scrubs the teeth. It is an automatic response, or a habituation, conditioning... Something you have done many times before. These patterns or habits are stored in your subconscious mind so you do not need to think or remember how to conduct your everyday life.

When you shift your attention from dealing with your environment to watching TV or writing a letter or fooling around on Facebook, you have now shifted your brain activity from a beta or alert level of brain activity to an alpha level, which is a light state of relaxation. You are not concerned with what is going on around you, unless someone calls your name or the phone rings. You are now focused upon the story on TV, or how you want to say something in a letter or scrolling through Facebook keeping up with friends and acquaintances.

You are also not fully aware of your body, it is in a comfortable position at the moment, it is still, so is your breathing, it is probably slow and paced, however you are unaware of this.

The alpha state or light state of relaxation is one of the levels you experience in hypnosis.

There are three basic levels of hypnosis:

☞ Light/alpha

☞ Medium > alpha/delta

☞ Deep/somnambulistic > delta/theta

You will experience what is called the hypnotic rhythm, in which you will travel through these states of relaxation, and attention. No one state is better than the other. You do not need to be at the deep state in order to benefit. Additionally, each time you enter hypnosis, it will be different every time.

A medium state of hypnosis is similar to waking up in the morning with no obligations to tend to, so you can just lay there, maybe still dreaming a little, aware of the sounds in your environment like birds chirping outside, or the sounds of people in the house, and you are so relaxed you don't know where the bed ends and you begin.

The deep or somnambulistic state of hypnosis is what everybody thinks what hypnosis is, it is like you fell asleep and just becoming aware of where you are or somebody is speaking.

Hypnosis is not something done to you, it is something in which you allow and engage in.

When you are relaxed, your mind communicates differently. When hypnosis is applied it can change a habit into a choice. Hypnosis works in direct proportion to your level of motivation. You cannot be hypnotized to do something you don't want to do! It must be a personal choice and personally desired. Hypnosis works with your level of motivation, no one else's.

If you compare hypnosis to a computer, you can see that both are capable of processing billions of bits of information. Hypnosis can help you rewrite these undesired habits into new programs that you can use in any way you choose. It can help you achieve whatever you want to consciously accomplish.

Your subconscious mind is an amazing tool, again, it is where your programming or conditioning automatically allows you to effortlessly do what you need to do, such as driving. Each time you get behind the wheel you do not need to relearn how to operate the vehicle, it's a conditioned behavior and without thinking, easily go about your business.

For the best results remember; hypnosis does not make you do anything. It simply helps you relax that compulsive or anxious feeling and reminds you of what you consciously want to do. Hypnosis is Natural.

Remember, hypnosis simply put is a change of conscious focus. We experience this normally throughout our day through daydreaming, zoning out in front of the T.V. or becoming deeply interested in a project. Hypnosis works from a heightened state of awareness, by balancing the conscious and subconscious mind.

Hypnosis is a state of intense focus. The key of modifying most behavior naturally exists in the subconscious. It takes cues from what we consciously concentrate and focus on repeatedly. Through hypnotherapy you can change habits, addictions and affect your state of health in a gentle yet potent manner that is not a quick fix, but a solution that is lasting and very effective.

People unfamiliar with hypnosis often ask: "Can I be Hypnotized?" Here are some simple facts; There are 4 types of people who are not good candidates for hypnosis:

1) Has a low IQ, under 70.
2) If there is a poor rapport with the hypnotist.
3) Persons diagnosed with psychosis.
4) Believe they are giving up control to the hypnotist.

Hypnosis or hypnotherapy is not mind control, if it was, I would invite you for a session, do an induction, then suggest you turn all of your assets over to me... then I would call you from that exotic island I own for our next session.

The higher your IQ or intelligence, the easier hypnosis works for you. We as hypnotherapist do not understand all the reasons of this fact, it may have to do with the ability to follow instructions.

Some people worry they might get stuck in hypnosis. You cannot get stuck... Have you ever got stuck in a daydream or sleeping?

Hypnosis works with the essence of your nature, which is truly powerful. You are self-actualizing.

The most important benefit of hypnosis is it eliminates substantially the discomforts or resistances both physically and psychologically attached to changing behaviors and addictions, such as withdrawal symptoms and anxiety that sometimes accompanies change. This allows you to relegate a negative/unproductive behavior to the past, "something you used to do that you simply do not do anymore." Like out-growing a pair of shoes, seamlessly you now move forward and onward with your life, dreams and aspirations. "You Are An Unending Horizon."

Hypnosis can by-pass automatic reactions or resistance, successfully reprogram past limiting beliefs, or as I call it, upgrading to a 2.0 system, childhood tapes, and shift this valuable energy toward your dreams and aspirations.

The truth of who you are lives here, within the subconscious, beyond your conscious limitations. The truth is that you are worthy of your dreams, your ambitions and your personal goals beyond whatever or whoever might have unintentionally programmed otherwise.

90-95% of our lives is controlled by the subconscious.

Conscious Mind:
10%

1) Analyzes
2) Thinks and plans
3) Short-term memory

Subconscious Mind:
90%

1) Long-term memory
2) Feelings and emotions
3) Habit patterns, relationship patterns, addictions
4) Involuntary body functions
5) Creativity
6) Developmental stages
7) Spiritual connection
8) Intuition

What is Cognitive Behavior Training

The Here and Now

Cognitive Behavior Training is a approach that addresses dysfunctional emotions, maladaptive behaviors and cognitive processes and contents through a number of goal oriented explicit systematic procedures. Most counselors and therapists working with patients dealing with anxiety and depression use a blend of cognitive and behavioral techniques. This technique acknowledges that there may be behaviors that cannot be controlled through rational thought. CBT is "problem focused" strategies to help address those problems.

CBT is effective for the correction of a variety of conditions, including mood, anxiety, personality, eating, substance abuse dis-orders. Many CBT treatment programs for specific dis-orders have been evaluated for efficacy; the health-care trend of evidence-based approaches where specific treatments for symptom-based diagnoses are recommended, has favored CBT over other approaches such as psychodynamic treatments.

CBT was primarily developed through an integration of behavior therapy or "behavior modification" with cognitive psychology research.

While rooted in rather different theories, these two traditions have been characterized by a constant reference to experimental research to test hypotheses, both at clinical and basic level.

Common features of CBT procedures are the focus on the "here and now", a directive or guidance role of the counselor or therapist, a structuring of the counseling sessions and path, and on alleviating both symptoms and patients' vulnerability.

Recent variants emphasize changes in one's relationship to maladaptive thinking rather than changes in thinking itself. Counselors or computer-based programs use CBT techniques to help individuals challenge their patterns and beliefs and replace "errors in thinking such as overgeneralizing, magnifying negatives, minimizing positives and catastrophizing" with "more realistic and effective thoughts, thus decreasing emotional distress and self-defeating behavior."

These errors in thinking are known as cognitive distortions. CBT techniques may also be used to help individuals take a more open, mindful, and aware posture toward them so as to diminish their impact. Mainstream CBT helps individuals replace maladaptive coping skills, cognitions, emotions and behaviors with more adaptive ones, by challenging an individual's way of thinking and the way that he/she reacts to certain habits or behaviors.

Modern forms of CBT include a number of diverse but related techniques such as exposure therapy, stress inoculation training, cognitive process training, cognitive training, relaxation training, dialectic training and acceptance and commitment.

CBT has six phases:
1. Assessment
2. Reconceptualization
3. Skills acquisition
4. Skills consolidation and application training

5. Maintenance

6. Post treatment and assessment

The reconceptualization phase makes up much of the "cognitive" portion of CBT.

There are different protocols with important similarities among them. Use of the term *CBT* may refer to different interventions, including self-instructions (e.g. distraction, imagery, motivational self-talk), relaxation and/or biofeedback development of adaptive coping strategies (e.g. minimizing negative or self-defeating thoughts), changing maladaptive beliefs about pain, and goal setting. Training is sometimes manualized, with brief, direct, and time-limited treatments for individual psychological disorders that are specific technique-driven.

CBT is used in both individual and group settings, and the techniques are often adapted for self-help applications. Some clinicians and researchers are cognitively oriented (e.g. cognitive restructuring), while others are more behaviorally oriented (e.g. in vivo exposure). Interventions such as imaginal exposure therapy combine both approaches.

Specific applications

CBT has been applied in both clinical and non-clinical environments to treat dis-orders such as personality conditions and behavioral problems. In depression and anxiety dis-orders concluded that "CBT delivered in primary care, especially including computer or internet-based self-help programs, is potentially more effective than usual care and could be delivered effectively by primary care counselors or therapists."

Emerging evidence suggests a possible role for CBT in the treatment of ADHD in coping with the impact of multiple sclerosis, sleep disturbances related to aging; and bipolar dis-order. CBT has been studied as an aid in the treatment of anxiety associated with stuttering. Initial studies have shown CBT to be effective in reducing social anxiety in adults who stutter.

CBT is effective for management of depression and quality of life.

In adults, CBT has been shown to have a role in the treatment plans for anxiety dis-orders, depression dis-orders; chronic low back pain, personality dis-order, psychosis, schizophrenia, substance abuse, depression, and anxiety associated with fibromyalgia and with post-spinal cord injuries.

There is some evidence that CBT is superior in the long-term to benzodiazepines and the nonbenzdiazepines in the treatment and management of insomnia CBT has been shown to be moderately effective for treating chronic fatigue syndrome.

In children or adolescents, CBT is an effective part of treatment plans for anxiety dis-orders; body dysmorphic dis-order, depression and suicidality, eating dis-orders and obesity, obsessive compulsive dis-order and posttraumatic stress dis-order as well as tic dis-orders, trichottilmania (hair pulling) and other repetitive behavior disorders.

For suicide prevention, it was found to be effective, feasible, and acceptable. CBT has also been shown to be effective for posttraumatic stress dis-order in very young children (3 to 6 years of age).

What's in a word

Let's experiment:

Say out loud, "I have a problem."

Now, notice how you feel, is there any tension in your body, your jaw, neck, back, belly? How are your energy levels, do you feel elated or oppressed?

Now, say out loud, "I have a challenge."

Notice how you feel, is there any tension in your body, your jaw, neck, back, belly? How are your energy levels, do you feel elated or oppressed?

Become aware of any difference in your body and energy between the two statements. Most people say when they state, "I have a problem," they feel parts of their body tense up, a feeling of weight, or oppression. Often a sense of powerlessness and fear or sadness also accompanies.

As remarkable, people report that when they state, "I have a challenge," they feel a sense of uplifting energy, they feel lighter and have a sense of 'I can do'.

How often do you interchange those specific words, "Problem and Challenge?" Have you even noticed how the words and language you use physically affects you?

The roots of language is to describe. Often our word descriptions arise from our perceptions, or could it be the other way around? Is it possible that the words we use to describe are creating our perception? Is it possible the words in language are empowering or disempowering you?

The simple graph is representative of the creation cycle and feedback system of human thought nature.

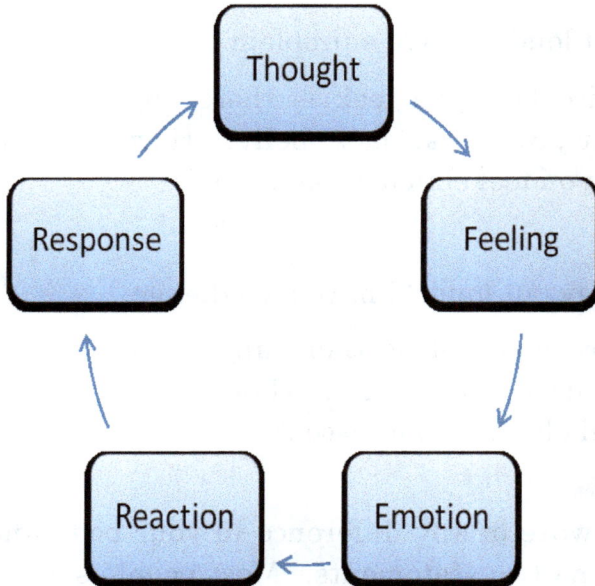

You have a mind, body and energy/spirit. Each and all react or respond to one another. For instance, if you <u>think</u> about a favorite food, it may produce a reaction of smiling, hunger, which is a <u>feeling</u>. While thinking of the last time you had that favorite food, and it was a pleasant or unpleasant experience, the combination of the thought and feeling combined draws up an <u>emotion</u>. By continuing to focus on the thoughts and feelings, it creates the motion of emotion.

You can think of the motion of emotions like ocean waves, ebbing in and then flowing out. Thoughts flow into and out of our minds constantly. As we continue to focus on the subject, that produces a reaction, which is habitual, something you have expressed many times before, such as feeling good or bad.

Photo By Jenny Harper LeBel

A response is different from a reaction. Reaction again is habitual, something you do not consciously think about, often we call that a 'knee jerk reaction.' A response is a conscious decision, such as deciding once the thought of your favorite food is to head to the refrigerator or store to obtain it.

In any given moment, we are reacting, responding or dismissing thoughts. Those thoughts we are reacting or responding to are those we choose to empower. To empower is to focus for a sustained period of time (seconds, minutes, hours). As you maintain focus, the combination of thought and feeling draws up emotions attached to the subject.

For example, you may recall eating your favorite food during a pleasant vacation, these positive memories unfold and you feel good, releasing endorphins in your body. Or, perhaps you had a negative experience while having your favorite food, you begin to feel anxious, releasing adrenaline which if you maintain that focus, continues to release an over load of adrenaline which produces the fight or flight or freeze response.

The fight or flight or freeze response is 200,000 years in the making. It is the brains survival instinct that creates an instantaneous (unconscious) reaction of either fighting a threat or running from a threat, and some people freeze in place, a form of hiding. Your instinctual survival mechanism is hard wired in the brain, and is produced by a <u>real</u> or <u>imagined</u> threat.

The good news is that anxiety and panic dis-order is not a disease as we currently understand the word, 'disease'. Here as well I hyphenate the word down to it's essential components, 'dis-ease'. Why? It is easier to digest, if you will, what we are specifically speaking of. Labels are designations, a description.

If you take these two words that can be labels, and break it down to it's essential nature, the actual meaning of these terms, you will begin to shift your thinking and/or beliefs associated with them. Why? Because when an authority figure, such as a doctor or therapist labels you with a disorder or disease, parts of you take on that label, in effect, you are a victim of...(fill in the blank).

The Fight or Flight or Freeze Response in the body

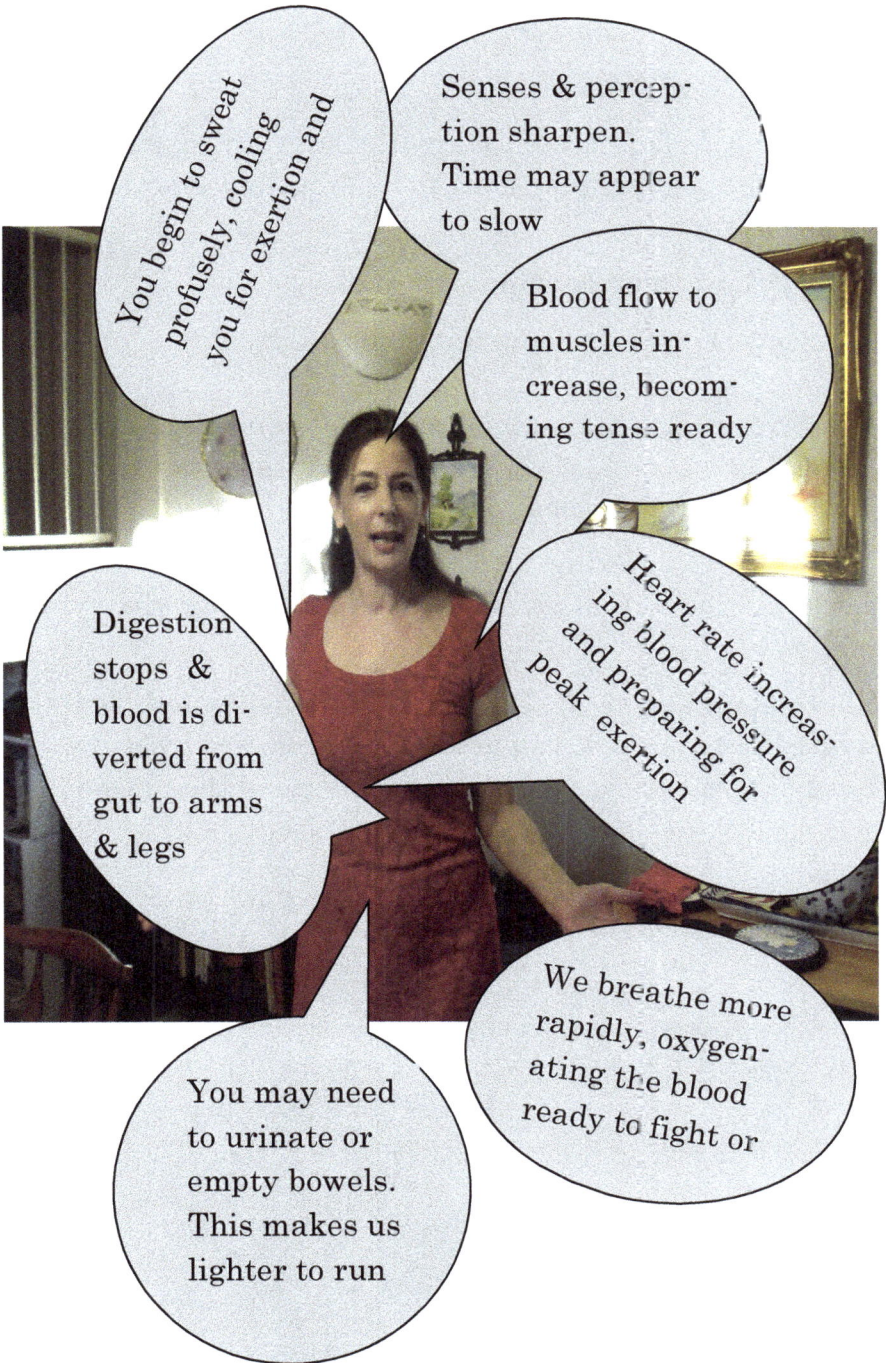

Notice the difference of how you <u>feel</u> as you read these words:

Disorder. Now, dis-order.

Disease. Now, dis-ease.

Our ideas, beliefs associated with the word together as a whole has a different thought, feeling and emotion connected to them.

A dis-order is merely things out of place.

A dis-ease is merely being uncomfortable.

Correcting or managing anxiety or panic does not take months or years of psychotherapy, it's concerns are right here in the present moment.

How? By re-ordering your thinking. It is what you are thinking about that is creating or provoking the symptoms.

There is a knowing in Tao: "If you are depressed, you are living in the past. If you are anxious, you are living in the future. If you are at peace, you are living in the present."

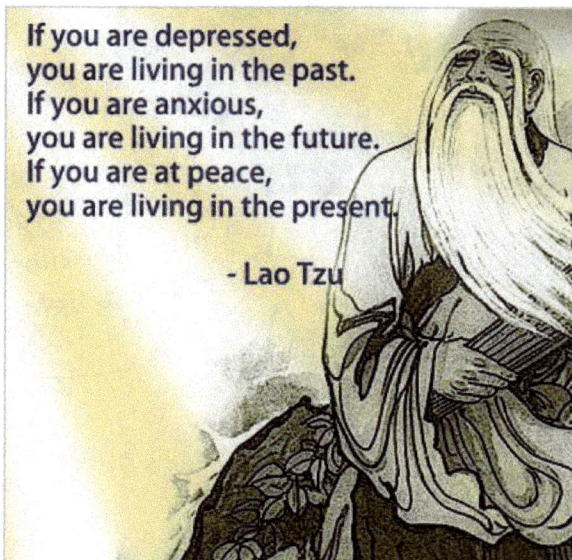

If you are depressed,
you are living in the past.
If you are anxious,
you are living in the future.
If you are at peace,
you are living in the present.

- Lao Tzu

What does the word; "Responsibility" mean?

I invite you to write it down, here…

_____

_____

_____

_____

_____

Now, the word 'responsibility' means: The ability to re-spond. That is it. So whatever you wrote down above is your perception and interpretation of the word, not the actual meaning.

We do this quite often, mis-taking meaning. Your subcon-scious knows the exact meaning of words, language. When used improperly, it will signal you often with a feeling. Re-member, we are a feedback system. If you find you are feeling uncomfortable, pay attention to what you just stated or thought. It was incongruent with your intention, so change the word to correctly reflect your intent, desire, true reflection.

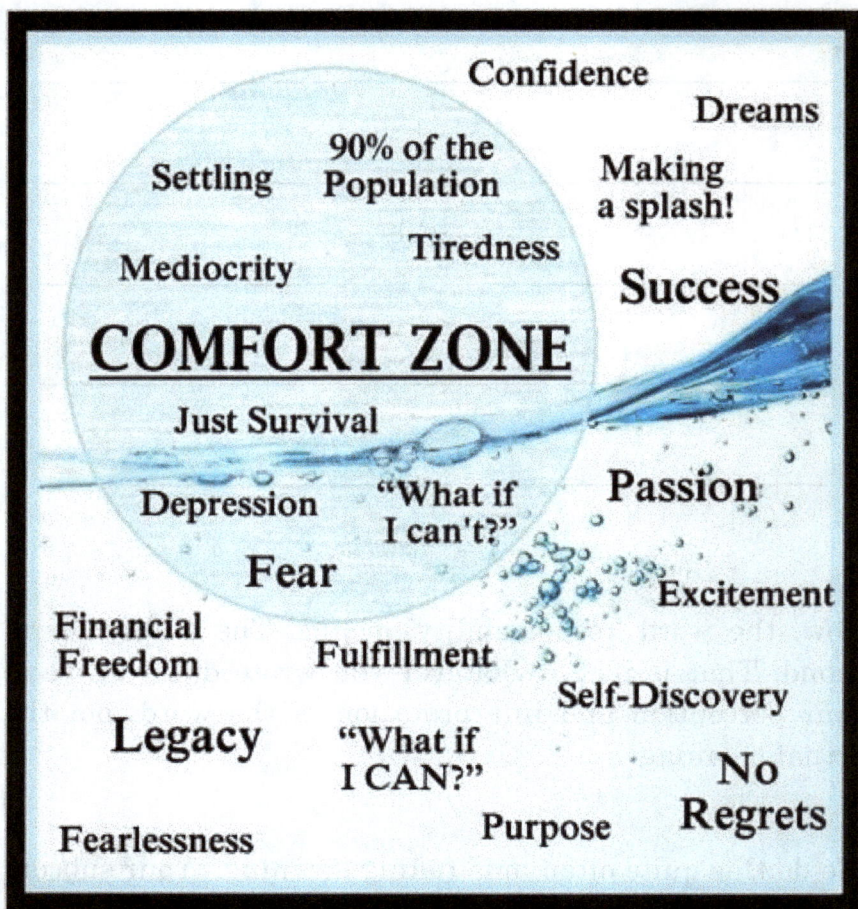

Confidence

Dreams

Settling   90% of the Population

Making a splash!

Mediocrity   Tiredness

Success

COMFORT ZONE

Just Survival

Depression   "What if I can't?"

Passion

Fear

Excitement

Financial Freedom   Fulfillment

Self-Discovery

Legacy   "What if I CAN?"

No Regrets

Fearlessness   Purpose

The Comfort Zone

As we pursue our goals and ambitions, any goal, trying on various new behaviors, methods and levels of outcome, we're going to feel and experience uncomfortable. Count on it! That is the process as we expand our personal boundaries. With this information in mind, changes can be handled with relative ease. Knowledge is power, and its utilization, your strength.

The comfort zone is the area of activities that we've done often enough to feel comfortable in doing. Anything new, different or untried lies outside our comfort zone, in the land of the uncomfortable or stressful

As we approach the edges of our comfort zone, we are at ease for the most part; experienced. Feelings of uneasiness begin to creep in, in which we feel one or more of five emotions:

Fear, Guilt, Enough-ism, Hurt feelings, Anger.

These are generally the feelings people have when they say; "I am uncomfortable."

With anxiety or panic or depression these feelings are exaggerated, magnified to where we find it difficult if not impossible to even think about doing some-thing different or untried, becoming immobilized and paralyzed by our thoughts and feelings created, considering changes.

For many people, the explanation, "I am uncomfortable" is sufficient reason not to do anything new or challenging. It is of little wonder than that these people seldom reach their dreams, change their lives. They Choose comfort over their goal. To reach our goals, to live our dreams we must CHOOSE, moment by moment to take steps in the direction of our dreams, no matter how uncomfortable we may feel. Reaching ones goals is not always comfortable. It is however satisfying. We are not speaking about intuition senses, we are speaking of fear.

When our thoughts automatically trigger a learned emotional reaction, Realizing we are in control, we can reprogram this process, these reactions empowers your abilities and resources in off-setting the physical/emotional changes and challenges that occur.

The subtle ways in which the comfort zone keeps us from our dreams are insidious (Adj; Causing harm in a way that is gradual, barely noticed. Latin *insidiosus,* from *insidiae* ambush, from *insidēre* to sit in, sit on, from *in-* + *sedēre* to sit) The comfort zone reacts with its "don't do it" messages long before we take a physical action. When we even think about doing something new and different or perhaps attempted prior, the comfort zone reacts. We have been programmed to do whatever it takes to avoid Fear, Guilt, Enough-ism, Hurt feelings and Anger.

The exaggerated physical reactions from anxiety or panic or depression are enough to totally avoid anything new or once done. Unfortunately, our personal world becomes smaller and smaller as our fear grows and burgeons into other areas of our lives, finding it difficult to trust ourselves in any responsible situation. So, we think about something else, something more comfortable...

One of the masks of the comfort zone is procrastination, a lack of motivation. Another mask is being a control freak.

At the very foundation of manifestation, at the level of Thought, the comfort zone seems to attack. We often unquestioningly, unconsciously follow our programming and focus on what is familiar, what is comfortable, safe.

In reality, the comfort zone is an important part of our built-in success mechanism. All the feelings of the comfort zone can be used for us, can be used to achieve our dreams and goals. We've simply been mis-programmed as to their proper use, even by so-called experts who may only deal with the symptoms of the comfort zone instead of how is this energy being misunderstood. We medicate or alleviate the discomfort, then try to figure out what is going on...

This "programming" takes place in childhood, through our environmental and parental examples, those who represent an authority figure and our own personal lack of knowledge that we are not in control of our own feelings, our thoughts.

As children, we need and were given boundaries. Example: Not to cross the street, it is dangerous!

A child does not know the difference between drinking poison or juice... For their own safety, they are taught and drilled; "If it is new, don't try it!". Our parents couldn't keep their eyes on us constantly, and we are trained essentially not to trust anyone or anything, it is dangerous. The strong feelings from the comfort zone arise are meant to protect you from harm.

As we become old enough to know the difference between that which is merely new and exciting and that which is genuinely physically harmful, no one draws us aside and says; "Oh, by the way, all those feelings of discomfort that you have been taught to avoid, you can start using those additional tools to get what you want."

It takes a while to do this re-programming. Fortunately on our way towards our dreams we'll have lots of opportunities... Each time fear or guilt, enough-ism or unworthiness, hurt feelings and anger surface, and they will, we can either CHOOSE to run from them or use them as the energy to take yet another step towards our dreams, goals and aspirations.

Recognizing we are creating these reactions physically through the mis-use of Thought will liberate us from a prison, a prison we never realized we hold the key to.

We have natural in-built resources to cope and contend with the exaggerated reactions; by breathing properly, slowly inhaling and exhaling; by changing the direction of thought, or completely focusing in new directions. (To our external environment). When we are reacting, it is as though we are sucked within ourselves, seemingly unable to extricate, pull ourselves from the spiraling feelings of powerlessness, uneasiness and discomfort.

It is our underlying Beliefs (what we believe is true or false) that create and continues these cycles or paralysis; of being in or out of control in and of our lives and feeling safe.

We are the Masters of our Minds, Captains of our Souls...

When "old" programming comes up, we must ask our-selves if our CHOICE is to continue to believe (exaggerated) limits or expand awareness.

Our CHOICE of Thought creates Feelings, our feelings ac-tivate Emotion, and it is Thought and Feeling combined that is the Motion of our Emotions.

☞ Fear becomes excitement, the energy to do our best in a new situation. The physical stamina or energy to mobilize physical action, displacing: Fight or Flight or Freeze.

☞ Guilt becomes the energy for making personal change, to understand our behavior, to change/understand/ challenge mis-taken beliefs about what our behavior "should" be most of the time. For addition insight, please refer to the article "Regret = Guilt & Depres-sion" towards the end of the book under the Articles Section.

☞ Enough-ism in its way keeps us on-track. We tell our-selves that we are worthy of our dream, and then let the feelings of unworthiness we have about pursuing all of the other dreams in the world to guide us to suc-cess. In essence, boundaries for consistency, focus. (Also a judgment, self-assessment...personal self-esteem)

☞ Hurt feelings remind us how much we care. If we did-n't care we wouldn't hurt. Hurt feelings remind us to turn back to caring, we use the energy to care for our-selves, thus healing whatever damage the hurt did.

Then we can direct or re-direct the energy towards our goals, dreams and aspirations.

☞ Anger is the energy to change. It informs us we need to focus to create or resolve. When anger is mis-used it tends to turn into destruction or depression; Depression is anger turned inside out.

What do I mean, depression is anger turned inside out? Simply put, we have a relationship with ourselves just like we do with other people. When we are disappointed by others for whatever reason; they didn't follow through, they broke a promise, we expected them to do something and it did not happen, we often feel betrayed, angry even disappointed. When we do the same things to ourselves, such as not following through, not meeting decided expectations, etc, we feel those same feelings, but within. With another person, sometimes we might display our anger and frustrations, sometimes we even end relationships if the person continues the same behavior. And we do the same thing to ourselves, except we are stuck with self. There is nowhere to go or hide. You are inside your own head perhaps still yelling or feeling betrayed, not trusting yourself or integrity or ability to move forward, and it turns against you.

Successfully re-programming/expanding the comfort zone is like learning to ride a bike. We can watch others as much as we like, but the place of true learning is on the bike. Yeah, you may fall as you are learning to balance; loose control, panic and do all the things we wanted to avoid by learning how to bike. It may seem for a while counter-productive. You may even notice you hear about bike accidents... this is a natural by-product of information and ways that we stick to what is comfortable! We are amazing, even if we don't realize it at first!

If however we stick to it, practice we learn to balance, steer, getting what we want; fun, recreation, exercise, rather than as a danger.

In order to expand the comfort zone to get what you want, you must feel what we currently call uncomfortable. It is part of the challenge of changing old limiting experience into new experience of open opportunity. In a few years you may automatically call fear excitement. For now however, it is fear and it is uncomfortable! Be willing to feel uncomfortable. Feel the fear and do it anyway! Take the next step towards your goals. Along the way you will begin seeing various emotions of the comfort zone as the friends they are, or an internal alert system signaling to you there is a incongruence in perception or old belief.

The comfort zone is like boundary lines, like a fence surrounding your property.

One of the benefits of realizing, pursuing our dreams is learning to use the comfort zone as the support system it truly is. The main benefit is realizing our dreams. The second is learning that no-thing is truly bad within ourselves: You learn that the world is not out to get you or you are self-defeating, broken, or weak.

You were merely mis-informed. With knowledge comes power. Power to be ourselves, to be self-actualizing, to live authentically. You begin to recognize you are truly the one who creates or recreates personal boundaries and feelings. It is a nightmare you can now awaken from.

You Are The Master of Your Mind, The Ruler of Your Body.

The present is your Point of Power, Where true CHOICE occurs.

The past cannot harm you, nor can the future.

You live, exist in the Present Moment.

How powerful to realize that the past is merely thought, and so too is the future.

Your reality is truly in the Here and Now.

How powerful you are, truly, that a "mere" thought can be so powerful to affect your physical body, your emotions.

A thought...

- It begins with a dream.
- Add preparation through diligent research.
- Add courage to initiate momentum without support.
- Add faith to meet ubiquitous resistance.
- Add passion when failures arise frequently.
- Add humor when passion temporarily drains.
- Add adaptability to adjust to the unknowable.
- Add patience as success slowly, occasionally unfolds.
- Add perseverance when backslides happen often.
- Add gratitude when reflecting upon the great process.
- Add service to share the experience of the process.
- Add another bigger dream, and restart.

~ Scott Sonnon
www.facebook.com/ScottSonnon

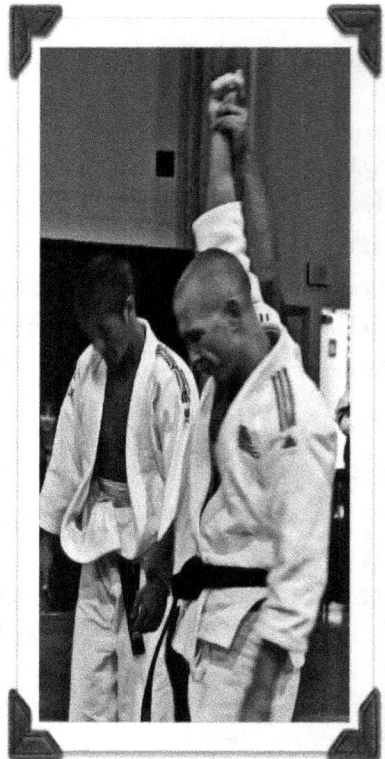

Points to ponder and profit

☞ Your point of power is always in the present.

☞ You are the creator and co-creator of your personal reality.

☞ You are a body, mind and spirit and is a feedback system.

☞ You are not separate from Divine Source, you are part and parcel.

☞ You are always programming your subconscious by what you think, say and how you hold your body.

☞ Every experience has and is an opportunity, it is always your choice to respond or react.

☞ You choose your thoughts.

☞ Words and language change or create perception.

☞ Most if not all issues arise from the notion "I'm not good enough".

☞ Good/bad, positive/negative, right/wrong are a perception.

☞ There is no Universal judge, it is all you.

☞ At your essential nature, you are whole, unique and valuable.

☞ As you trust yourself, you honor life, Universe in the highest form humanly possible.

☞ Life is not about perfecting or being perfect, you already are, it is about experience.

☞ You cannot fail, but you can delay.

☞ Life is a series of lessons, and until you get it, the same lesson/experiences will repeat.

```
N C G B G E N E R O U S L Y T R U S T Y U T L T
B O I N A F O R T R U T H F U L A F F L A R Y R
L M V Y L L U F E T A R G T R E A T L S B E L U
E P Y W H O A A C C A G R A T E F U E U E A E S
S L B L J O Y N L A T B R O Y T R U S O Y T T T
S E A E L T R U C Y R T U L E X P E R I O Y E F
Y T L T R A H I L E U E E N S O X O U N U O L B
O E A B R V C L F O Y T C S D P E G O O R E P L
U M N Y V U U I E L A O C G R A I J Y M S R M E
R P C I L F S G T I E S U E A V N S E R E U O S
S O E Y H T O T D S F S S R E B A T U A L R C S
E W Y T H E N E Y L A S R Y S M T O L H F T V Y
L E U C A E M A E O Y I O U Y E Y L A Y R R A O
F R F O R M R X I O U U S Y O E L O V B A E L U
T Y O M I A C C U D R R E U V Y R F I L D A U B
E O R P L C G R J S A L S I H E E Y M E I T E A
E U G L O O S O E E E R G E O T O V M S A Y Y L
M R I E V E Y L E M P R O U L O N S O S N O O A
P S V T L F F L O V O T R U L F U E I L T U U N
O E E F U N H A R F V T R E A T Y O U R S E L F
W L F L E S R U O Y T P E C C A C O M P L E T E
E F L Y L O V E Y O U R Y T C O M P L E T E U A
R Y Y L T N E D I F N O C B L E W H O L E H E A
Y U W H O L E H E A R T E D L Y B A L A N C E L
```

Strike a line or circle around words in grid. Words & word-lines are upward, backward vertical & horizontal.

- Be Yourself
- Forgive Yourself
- Bless Yourself
- Empower Yourself
- Truthfully
- Completely
- Abundantly
- Immediately
- Accept Yourself
- Treat Yourself
- Trust Yourself
- Give Yourself
- Gratefully
- Generously
- Confidently
- Enthusiastically
- Value Yourself
- Balance Yourself
- Love Yourself
- Express Yourself
- Joyfully
- Harmoniously
- Wholeheartedly
- Radiantly

Bottom line

As previously mentioned, the core root issue of anxiety dis-orders is feeling safe and in control in or of your world. Something has unseated your sense of center, of balance, of control. Often it comes down to your sense of self confidence. Do you compare yourself to others? The only time comparing yourself to another human being is when you are *aspiring* to their example. Otherwise it is an exercise in lying essentially. Why do I say this? Because there has never been anyone like you before, nor will there be anyone like you to come. You are a unique individual, with talents, strengths, quirks that cannot be replicated, ever, by anyone else. You are not any better or worse than anyone else. If you believe so, this is a lie you are selling yourself, and the price is astronomically high.

Our perception is based on what we believe. Our beliefs are based on experiences and what we are taught in early childhood. We reinforce our perceptions through the words and language we habitually speak, think, as well as through body language, how we are holding ourselves, body posture as pervious mentioned. I have a list of five particular words to either avoid, reframe or make sure you are using properly.

Hope ~ Wish ~ Can't ~ Should ~ Try

☞ Hope = Non-commitment

Hope is a very important attribute of the human experience. We need to hope things get better, but if you are merely hoping and not being proactive, taking some form of action to make the necessary changes you are misusing the word. You are living by default, not intent.

☞ Wish = Equals disempowerment

Wish is very close to hope, however, if you are wishing for change, perhaps you need a raise at work and wish the boss would see all of your efforts, but not speaking up and asking your boss and stating the extra efforts, more likely than not, you will not receive a raise.

Did you know 80% of bosses expect you to approach them for a raise?

☞ Can't = I won't

This is a very misused word, and more often than not we use can't attempting to spare someone's feelings or to be politically correct, think they may disappoint or even anger. People who have issues honoring their time and self, who have difficulty saying 'no' to another will use can't instead of no.

We have two sacred things solely and wholly that belong to each individual: one, our thoughts. No one knows exactly what we are thinking unless we disclose it through speech, writing, expressions. If this were not true we would not need a justice system.

Second are our feelings. No one knows exactly what you are feeling. We can empathize, sympathize as we may have had a similar experience... ever have someone say to you; "oh, you don't really feel that way." Did it anger you?

Pay close attention to these last two words

☞ Should = Procrastination

The word 'should' is an evil word... especially if you do not follow through. Should is the gateway to procrastination and leads to the threshold of depression. I say, never 'should on yourself, it can get messy'.

When you use the word 'should', more often than not you are acknowledging that something needs to be done or attended to. Such as you observe the garbage needs to be taken out perhaps while watching tv or passing by, and say to yourself, I should take out the garbage... then perhaps make an appointment with yourself... I will take out the garbage at the next commercial, or on my way out the door in the morning, then you get home and see that you forgot to take out the garbage, and then those choice words we have for ourselves begin spewing... you know those words we say and call ourselves when we feel betrayed, angry or disappointed by ourselves, those words that if another human being said to us would end up with a bloody nose, or if someone we cared about said to us would deeply hurt...

You know, we have a relationship with ourselves just like we do with other people. I'll get back to that...

In order to shift procrastination, we have to stop shoulding on ourselves, and follow through. So, when you get home and see that the garbage is still there, put down your things, no thought, no judgments, no calling yourself names, simply tie up the garbage and take it out.

Think about it, when was the last time someone cajoling or yelling or calling you nasty names motivated you?

Remember, you first need to change your perception, then you're thinking automatically follows.

☞ Try = Permission to fail

The word 'try' is a brilliant word for anyone under the age of 10... why, well, because when we are under the age of 10 we tend to be little perfectionists; we are coloring a picture and go outside the line or we are practicing our letters and we make a mistake, and some children become upset and then angry. When we are young, we seek approval, validation and acceptance from our parents and/or teachers, peers... Then at some point a teacher or parent will come up to us and say: "If at first you don't succeed, try try again..." this gives us permission to fail.

We need to fail before we become successful. My Grandmother used to say it takes 100 times drawing a rose before we get it right.

So failure is important as we develop and mature.

However, after the age of 10, we do not want to give ourselves permission to fail, we want to give ourselves permission to succeed, so, instead of saying I will 'try', you change it to, "I will do my best."

If you think about it, aren't we doing our best we can with what we know in any given moment?

Most people do not awake in the morning and decide they are going to be a miserable failure... most of us, there are those few....out there...

Think about it, when driving in your car, going from point A to point B, say coming home from work or school, the store...

...most of us only have the intention of arriving/completing the journey. Most of us do not intend to say, cut someone off, or miss a turn signal, intentionally irritating other drivers. Sometimes we just become inattentive, or are distracted, or working with the skill level we are at. We all have these moments. Keep this in mind the next time you are behind the wheel and feel irritated or frustrated by the traffic. We are all just working on getting home... or maybe rushing because a loved one is sick or in the hospital. Extend a little patience to others and to yourself. Most of us are doing the best we can with what we know in any given moment.

When you habitually state to yourself; "I'll try", you are giving yourself a 50/50 chance at success... I like those odds with a lottery ticket, but not in life!

Your subconscious knows exactly what that word means... Many of us have had the experience of asking a teacher; "How do I spell the word 'discipline'? And you get the response, 'go look it up in the dictionary'... yeah but teacher, I don't know how to spell it! Yeah yeah, you'll figure it out... so, you go to the dictionary, begin thumbing through the pages, and eventually come to the word 'dis-ka-pline'... dis-ka-pline? Then you read the meaning of the word, discipline... this is now locked into your subconscious mind. So if you misuse words and language, which programs and directs your subconscious, you may find yourself achieving the same results even though you are working very hard for changes in whatever, a situation, state of mind, feelings...

So, change the odds, state; I Will do my best!

You are not your thoughts. You simply pick n choose any random thought going through your mind which do one of two things: Empower you (in control) or Disempower you (out of control)

Say there are three different types of thought: the first type are those that go through your mind from the moment you pop out of the womb to the moment you become worm food. For example; through your five senses you are constantly downloading information (what you see, hear, taste, touch, smell) on a conscious and unconscious level. Anything and everything.

Actually, I think that the difference between regular people and genius is that they can access this information more easily, fluidly.

You are truly an uper duper super computer!

Random thoughts go through your mind, you pick one to focus on. Like kind thoughts follow like kind thoughts. So, if a scary or fearful thought is what you chose to focus on, you will create a feeling. Or you are in a conversation talking about favorite desserts...you say I adore a flourless chocolate cake, another says I have the best lemon cheesecake, another says fresh vanilla bean ice cream is the best... a giraffe will not enter your mind or the conversation, Your thoughts and feeling combined create the motion or cycle of emotion.

Second kind of thought: you and another person are having a conversation. From that conversation a new thought arises.

Third kind of thought: those are the thoughts I call the ones out in the ethers...such as you think of a friend and soon after you receive a call, text or email.

A personal story of Self Esteem

Upon my journey of dealing with and correcting my anxiety dis-order, I would have these bouts of depression. I couldn't understand where it was coming from? I had a wonderful family, healthy child, a house and general comforts. I would have these moments or days where I felt lower than a worms belly. I would sit at my desk pondering, wondering where all this came from, especially after all of the inner self work I was doing.

I remember as I asked myself for the millionth time, why do I feel this way, where is this coming from, a memory arose from my youth which I completely dismissed. Some time down the road another episode would occur, and the same pondering at my desk, and again this early memory... this time I did not dismiss it and decided to allow it to come to full consciousness and see if it had a clue or answer. (If you can pose a question, you have the answer)

... I am a little girl, maybe 4 years old. My father is calling for me from the kitchen. I run into the kitchen happy as my father is standing in the middle of the room with his hands upon his hips. I stand in front of him and he looks down at me and then points his finger in my face asking me angrily; "Who are you?" I was a little confused, but cheerfully answered; "I am Kathy." Again, now raising his voice and sternly pointing in my face asks; "Who are you!" I knew there was no right answer, I knew I was going to get a beating, and I didn't know what to say. So, gulping, I said softly; "Kathy." He then violently pointed his finger in my face and said; No, you are nothing and you will never be anything, you are nothing."

Well, I sat there at my desk and took a big wow breath and thought to myself, well, that explains things! My father, my authority figure, my god at the time pronounced I would never be anything, I was a nothing. My mind absorbed this, and I could see why so much of my life I spun my wheels, always ending up failing, starting all over again and again and again.

Fortunately I knew what to do. I needed to shift the emotional energy from that experience. So what I did is I would replay the memory all the way through, with the exception that I, as a grown woman stood behind little Kathy. And when father finished saying I will be nothing, I encouraged the child to look him in the eye and state; "I am Kathy and I will be anything I want when I grow up." I needed to do this several times until the emotional charge drained and was neutralized. It is called desensitization... it is a technique used for trauma and PTS.

Once the emotional charge was released, so was the events of depression and sense of worthlessness.

Now an interesting aside note: There is a saying; "that when you heal yourself, you heal a part of the world." I learned about a year later that something shifted with my father. My sister says he seems more peaceful and kinder. He doesn't loose his temper quite so quickly. I do not believe this to be a coincidence. My father and I were cordial, and spoke a few times throughout the years on holiday's and birthdays. I never mentioned what I had discovered or what I was doing. We primarily spoke of the weather, a favorite subject of mine.

Somehow, by healing my psyche, a part of him healed too.

Do you react or respond when challenges or the unexpected arise?
Good thing to be mindful of...
I see things as inherent opportunities if one lets go of expectations.
Was the power going down inconvenient?
Perhaps. Went outside to take the opportunity of the lights being off.
to gaze at stars often obscured.
The stillness of the night was ever pervasive. soothing and an
experience I often do not seek. enjoying the sound of the spoken word on the radio
or tv or conversations on fb.

Often, as I let go of expectations, plans, step back and reassess.
a plethora of possibilities as a western horizon, expansive. near limitless

Kate
Ellis,echt

YOUR VOICE COMMANDS YOUR MIND, BODY & SPIRIT

Learn the true meaning of each word, the root and the original intention. Find the cousins to each word, say it, feel it, which one will move you forward in your own life?

ENERGY + VIBRATION = MATTER

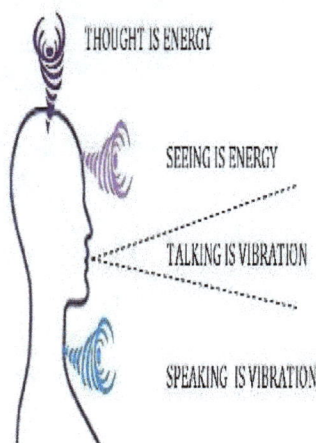

I can't		• Will literally stop growth
I won't		• Will literally put a block in your way
It's hard	=	• Can not is a command to self
I Don't Believe		• Will literally stop you from achieving anything in your life
I'm a skeptic		• Is a taught behavior that is a conditional to hold a person back
I don't like it		• Stops a person from learning
		• Stops a person from gaining intellect (IQ)

THOUGHT IS ENERGY

SEEING IS ENERGY

TALKING IS VIBRATION

SPEAKING IS VIBRATION

Try		• Try and you will do it over and over and over never get to the end
Trying		• Puts a block in your way
I can try		• Try is a command to self
I'm trying	=	• Try and trying is a taught behavior that is a condition to hold a person back
I will try		• It has very little or no results
I will attempt		• It is like running a race with no end
		• It is never ending
		• It is repetitious

THOUGHTS + VOICE = REALITY

Help the self by Walking the Absolute Truth of your own life, Meditate & Pray...Keep thoughts, actions & words positive...Be self empowered and use the tools presented in a good way

I can		• Literally promotes growth
I am		• Can is a command to self
I believe		• Allows your wants, needs and desire to come true
It is done	=	• Is a behavior of using good words
I can do it		• It is unconditional and moves a person forward in life
I can do anything		• When you know inside you can do it your body needs to hear it
		• Your body reacts to key words

Made with unconditional love:
Barbara M. Moreau, Angel who dances on the Clouds
Frank J. Austin, Manyhorses (Teacher)

What to do when you become
Anxious or Panic

Become aware, there are varying levels of anxiety. Sometimes it is a feeling of un-ease, being uncomfortable in your own skin or the sensation of (intense) fear.

☞ Number one, avoid caffeine in all forms! If you are feeling even slightly anxious caffeine will cause you to feel even more nervous, it is a stimulant, you do not need any further stimulants, it is far better to seek a mint product such as tea, a breath (spear) mint, even chewing gum. Chamomile is also excellent for it's soothing, calming effects, light on sugar.

☞ Water is your biggest ally; it flushes any toxins built up in your system, such as medications, what you in-gested the previous day as well as the adrenaline re-leased. It is best to sip room temperature water, it works fastest and bestest.

☞ You may perhaps awake feeling anxious. Take in a long, slow deep breath through the nose, pause for a moment, then slowly exhale through your mouth as though you are blowing soap bubbles or whistling as you give yourself directive messages: I am safe; This is a good day; I am well, All Is Well. etc.

☞ You may want to spend a few minutes simply breath-ing in a controlled manner as you hold a smile for 30-45 seconds. Why? Because the act of smiling releases the chemicals in your brain associated with happiness, joy, comfort. I suggest taking a pen or pencil, placing it across your teeth and bite gently it so it creates a smile.

☞ Be aware if you are thinking about the things you have on your schedule of the day. If you do not have a list written, create a list, do not keep these thoughts running through your mind. If you write things down, you can refer to the list and not worry about remembering everything you have to do. As you go about your day, strike a line through the items you have accomplished, and if needed, add to your list as you move through your day. You will find that not only do you not have your mind clogged up with things to remember, but you will find you are easily recalling, without a sense of urgency or anxiety about the things on the list.

<u>To Do List</u>

+ Bank

__ Pick up milk

__ Make dentist appointment

__ Make dinner

+ Pay phone bill

__ Reply to emails

☞ Remember, your emotions are responding to the combination of thoughts and feelings combined. So as you utilize these tools, you A) gain control of your thoughts. Controlled breathing allows the layers of thoughts to relax to just a few thoughts, which you are reinforcing by choosing exactly what to think, specifically directing your thoughts instead of being directed by them. You are not your thoughts. You are the one picking and choosing which to empower or focus upon. You do not need to believe every thought you become aware of; produced or habitual.

B) As you slow the content and layers of thought, your feelings automatically follow. Your feelings are produced by the content of thought (conscious or unconscious). If you are focusing on things that may not be within your control, what kind of feelings do you think will follow? Thoughts of a specific content are grouped together, or what I call 'like kind thoughts'. In your mind is a sort of filing cabinet. In this cabinet is an organization system such as file folders. Consider that you have in that cabinet a file with the heading; Fear. Clustered nearby would be other files that are similar in content: Sadness; scary things; anger; hate; problems; worry; out of my control, etc.

Think about when you were say, with other people and a conversation starts with 'the scariest things that ever happened to me'. Each person will recount their experience. Often you can relate or had something very similar occur. You will find that as you focus on those experiences, like kind additional experiences will come to the forefront of your mind, and you will then share those stories, as well as the other people and their experiences.

When you focus on something negative, (emotionally charged) other like kind negative memories will be easily recalled, as well as the feelings and then emotions associated with those experiences. Emotions produce chemical changes in your body. You may feel tense, unwell. The longer you dwell on a specific line of thinking, the feelings re-created will set the stage for the motion of emotions, releasing powerful brain chemicals and hormones.

This is way cool! Why you may ponder, what is so cool about feeling terrible? Because you created it and you can un-create it... by shifting the focus of your thoughts. Thoughts are as powerful as the air we breathe. Air is invisible; thoughts are also invisible. Air, it allows life. Thoughts, allow the contentment in our life. Air, a force that can cool the body on a hot day with a gentle breeze or blow down a house. Thoughts, a force that has created everything you can see all around you, and this book in which you hold in your hands.

Incorrect thinking are not the only issues related to anxiety. Often many medicines will produce anxiety or panic dis-order such as some blood pressure medications. Become proactive and read the inserts, speak to your pharmacist, they are far more knowledgeable more often of that of the prescribing doctor.

Additionally, thyroid disease, specifically a hypothyroid cause similar symptoms of panic. Electrolyze imbalances, low blood sugar (hypoglycemia).

There are two simple home test you can do to see if you may have a hypothyroid; Right after awakening in the morning, take your auxiliary temperature (armpit) before you move or get out of bed. If it is below 97.6 f you may have an underactive thyroid. I suggest a Naturopathic test above a regular western doctor test, due to the fact that western blood testing does not always properly assess a slightly underactive thyroid, or more precisely, interpretation of results.

The second thing you can do to see if you have a hypothyroid condition is to take a supplement called Kelp. One once a day, especially if you have been diagnosed with depression. You will feel immediate relief. Mind you, only one kelp tab a day. It is high in iodine which may be a missing, vital nutrient in your diet.

I had a client who presented with a panic dis-order. He had had one when he was a kid for a period of time. He was experiencing agoraphobia after witnessing his beloved aunt die from a heart attack and then the following day his grandfather died of a heart attack upon finding out his daughter had died. His anxiety symptoms made him run back into the house. After a while, he realized the trigger, and forced himself to go outside for a little time. Then descend the stairs to the street and calmed himself. Then he began walking down the block, discarding the intense messages telling him to go back home. He dismissed those thoughts over and over again. He allowed the sensations of fear and discomfort to dissipate. With a little time, courage and entertaining his desire to be outside and be a ten year old boy he learned how to manage then over come it.

40 years later, after some medical issues, he was prescribed a different blood pressure medication. Shortly afterward he began experiencing debilitating panic attacks. I helped him out, but it would re-manifest a few days later or after leaving the office driving down the street. Quite odd! Never had a client re-experience a panic attack after providing the corrective sessions. I went into serious investigative mode and discovered that a mistake in his medication had been made. He was receiving medication primarily prescribed after heart surgery, and then the medication is changed at discharge to something that does not need to be monitored in hospital.

When this information was brought to the doctors attention, they immediately changed his blood pressure medication, and the panic attacks ended.

I had another client who was also taking a commonly prescribed medication for acid reflux. She developed an awful spastic bowel issue, to the point she would think she was passing gas, and it wasn't. Many times she would have to return home, bath and change hers clothes. It was getting to the point she was afraid to leave the house. Health related issues all have an emotional component, she was seeing me for this issue. Again, it would clear up for a while, then re-emerge! It took quite a while of our combined investigation to discover it was the acid reflux medication she was taking that created this side-effect. She discontinued the medication and the issue resolved.

☞ Do not discount your diet in relation to your physical and emotional health. If you are having an anxious day, you will want to avoid high sugar, or any sugar content. It is what.... A stimulant. Carbohydrates such as breads, pasta. These turn into a sugar in your system. Certain fruits, such as oranges, grapes are high in sugars and carbohydrates. The best fruit are apples. Apples are low in sugars as well as has a calming effect on the stomach. It also balances the acids and if you have issues with appetite due to anxiety, it will prepare your stomach to eat. Banana's are also good for being nutrient dense and easy on the stomach. Pay attention to how you feel after you eat.

☞ Processed foods, many froze meals, many fast food are high in sugar, salt, carbohydrates and preservatives you may inadvertently be allergic or sensitive. Notice how you feel after eating these foods. Eliminate those foods from your diet. Note that a diet low in nutrients will actually cause you to gain weight and increases mood swings. You have more neurotransmitters in the gut then the brain. Diet effects mood.

☞ It is too easy these days, in the 21st century to be sedentary. This is counter productive to in the least, 200,000 years of homo-sapiens evolution. We are of the earth, and our bodies have developed in direct relationship with the earth, the moon, the sun and yes, influences of the planets. Did you know exercise is cumulative? If you break down a 30 minute routine of walking or yoga into five minute segments throughout the day, is the same benefits of a sustained 30 minutes of exercise. Movement regulates your elimination system, sweats out toxins and keeps the body toned.

There are certain vitamins our body does not produce, but needs to be created by exposure to certain elements, such as sunshine. It takes about 15 minutes of sunshine for our bodies to produce vitamin D. It is essential to our overall health, no vitamin D, equals brittle bones and other nasty things. Sunshine also produces good brain chemicals. We need a certain amount of sunlight in order to be emotionally healthy.

People who live in areas with days upon days without sunshine have issues with SADD dis-order (Seasonal Affective Disorder). When we spend a little time in sunlight, it allows the brain chemicals to balance themselves, and it works through the eyes and the back of the knees. Yes, the back of the knees!

If you are in an area with days of limited sunlight, get a full spectrum light bulb and place it where you live most. Also, incandescent bulbs are better than florescent. Also a fresh Hyacinth plant aids in uplifting spirits and energies including peppermint.

Why? Because being tired, you may be allergic to florescent light. How? Well, older florescent light bulbs begin to flicker as they age, like a strobe light, most people cannot see it, but it can make your brain feel you are in a trance, tired, lethargic. Back in the 1950's or 1960's school systems began discovering children's test scores were going down, and they couldn't figure out why. Then they discovered that the schools with the worst performance all had only florescent lighting. When they added incandescent and more natural lighting, test scores improved markedly. There was at some point a law instituted that all schools had to have a mixture of these types of lighting.

☞ Another interesting technique is to imagine a violet or

velvety blue light surrounding you, or streaming down through the top of your head down to your feet. The vibration of this color creates a safe, calming sensation. Light has a vibration, even imagining it... remember, it is Your imagination creating the sense of threat, a thought... so if a thought of a real or imagined threat can create the physiological changes in your body, so can your thoughts shut anxiety and panic down.

I had shared my techniques with my professional organization, The Arizona Society for Professional Hypnosis, and had mentioned the color technique. Not long after that a colleague was in a grocery store and her blood sugar began to drop, and she began to panic big time. She recalled the information I shared and imagined the violet light and immediately shut down a full blown panic attack, and did not feel that sense of shakiness or exhaustion following.

The Mesencephalon is the mid-brain, a portion of the central nervous system associated with vision, hearing, motor control, sleep/wake, arousal (alertness) and temperature regulation.

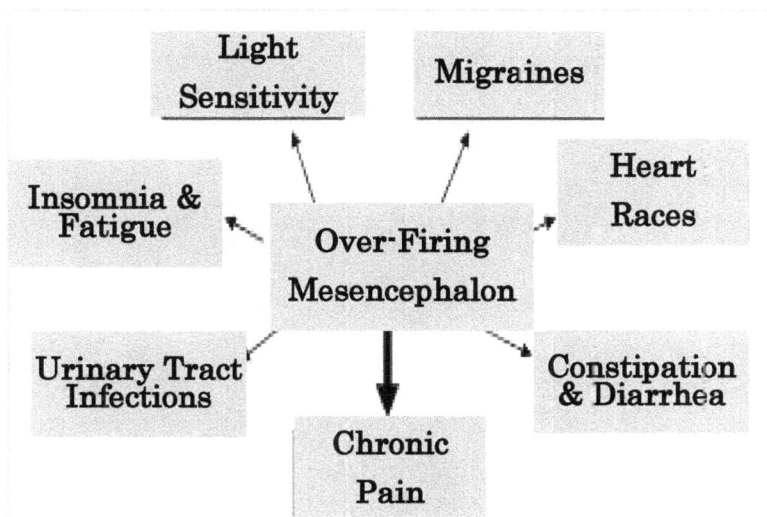

Persistent or chronic anxiety are more often than not responsible for the above issues. After enough time, the digestive issues can result in IBS, Crohns disease and other nasty things.

Lastly, I highly recommend journaling, writing down your thoughts of the day (totd) as I call them. It is a way to release and relieve pressure, and things squirreling round n round your mind. A major benefit is that you can look back through what your have penned down and become more succinctly aware of your true feelings. Sometimes we are so close to the issues, we fail to see important insights to our true feelings, recognize patterns that may be sabotaging our best efforts, such as an attitude expressed through words, which reflects what you are focused upon subconsciously.

I AM

Enough, Humour, Giving, Valuable, Bold, Serious, Creative, Loved, Evolving, Courageous, Wisdom, Divine, Honest, Grounded, Imperfectly perfect, Empathetic, a Dancer, Caring, Passionate, Love, Loyal, a Survivor, Responsible, Mischievous, Considerate, Unique, Me, Learning everyday, Worthy, Trusting, Generous, Serenity, Emotional, Playful, Kindness, a Volunteer, Life, an Encourager, Holy, Compassionate, Powerful, Healthy, Supporting, Abundance, Warm, Fun, Passion, Loving, Patient, Present, Special, Kind, Happy, a Work of Art, a Phoenix, Hard-working, Sensitive, Aloha, Sincere, Trustworthy, Eternal, Infinite, Funny, Complex, Strong, Silly, Blessed, Patient, Transforming, Lovingable, Awesome, Vivacious, Lucky, a Connector, Resourceful, Mother

102

Reset Button

You are running late, negotiating traffic, it slows to a crawl and time is ticking, people are waiting for you. Other drivers all of a sudden become idiots who can't drive. Your phone is dead, no way to inform you are in route. As the moments that feel like hours tick by, you are becoming more and more irate, thinking others will be annoyed, inconvenienced or perhaps even angry with you, your thoughts are racing, blood pressure increasing and you're getting angrier.

Finally you realize there is no getting around this. You are late. There is nothing you can do about it. And then the most extraordinary things happen upon this realization; your body sighs deeply. A new thought arises, deciding what you are going to do once you arrive at your destination, and feel more in control.

The sigh is your personal calming mechanism gifted to you by mom and nature. Yes, mom. When you were an infant and fussing to sleep, mom would sooth you at first, perhaps sing a song, rock you in her arms until you drifted into sleep. A few months later, as you fussed to sleep, mom would let you fuss, cry for a while, allowing you to find your own comfort zone, calmness, and you now have the tools to fall asleep. If you ever watched a baby discovering the comfort zone, you would observe it taking a deep breath, then drifting off to sleep 30 seconds later.

We all have this innate ability to calm and center

ourselves, more often than not, you do not even realize you are doing it. By consciously utilizing the body sigh, you are able to calm and center yourself within 3-5 slow, deep breathes. I call this the "Reset Button" technique. Mindfully become aware of any tension in your jaw, shoulders and stomach or lower back, and release it. Move your jaw side to side, raise your shoulders towards your ears and let them gently drop, let your belly relax, then inhale through the nose, pause a moment or two, then release through the mouth twice as slowly as your inhalation, repeat 3-5 times. It is best to inhale through the nose and exhale through the mouth.

The benefits of practicing this are multifaceted: Relaxing the muscles allows you to release any emotions you are holding onto. The deep breath delivers nutrient rich oxygen to the brain allowing it to clear thinking for a moment, which then allows you to choose what thoughts you focus upon. You can do this anywhere, anytime, whether sitting, standing, lying down. Most importantly, it delivers you back to your center, you gain control of your mind and what you choose to focus on and release stress and anxiety. Through the Reset Button you are gaining control of your autonomic/sympathetic nervous system which controls your breathing rate, heart rate, sweat rate, bleeding rate, etc. When you are in the throes of anxiety or panic your adrenal glands secreting adrenaline have been activated creating the symptoms. This is your goal is to regain control of these systems thereby gaining control and managing the symptoms. Practice the Reset Button twice a day for no particular reason, then as needed. As needed is feeling stressed or jittery. You are the Master of your Mind, Ruler of your Body.

Expanding a little on emotions in the muscles: If you ever

visited a massage therapist, they will tell you that "issues are in the tissues." And this indeed is true. Emotions can become entrapped within the muscles and tissues, and by consciously releasing key points of tension, you can then allow release of not only chronic physiological tension, but emotional as well by being conscious of your posture, tension in your body. It speaks a truth of the moment, and as you become aware that you are a feedback system, body and mind... you can heal and balance yourself.

Further on the point of muscle tension entrapping emotions; Doctors who deal with cosmetic medicine administering Botox have inadvertently discovered that when the Botox is used to calm the furrows on the forehead, patients reported their depression lifted and disappeared. Currently this is being investigated in regards to Botox being used to treat depression.

There are arguments on many sides, some clinicians stating it is because the patient feels better about the way they look, and feels happier. The debate continues. It can be both. Regarding my work and practice and experience, the release of chronically held tensions allows the accompanying emotions to release and thus dissolve.

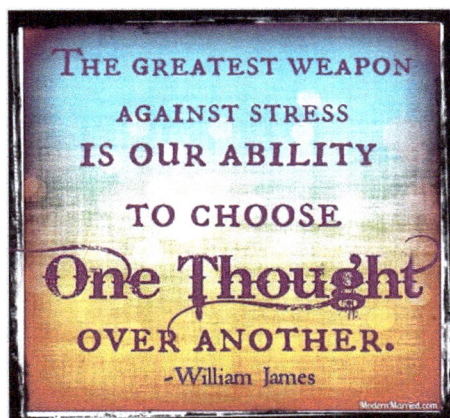

THE GREATEST WEAPON
AGAINST STRESS
IS OUR ABILITY
TO CHOOSE
One Thought
OVER ANOTHER.
-William James

For a seed to achieve its greatest expression, it must come completely undone. The shell cracks, its insides come out and everything changes. To someone who doesn't understand growth, it would look like complete destruction.

Cynthia Occe

Breathing

Breathing is easy until you begin to notice it.

Notice your breathing, but do not attempt to control it.

This can be a hefty idea, for, once you begin to notice and observe your breath, something inside may have you sigh, that is, to breathe in deeply and let it out in a quick short burst!

This is a good thing.

The body naturally sighs to refresh the brain.

One breath in, a pause, then a release out, clears the mind. Think of a time you were running late for an appointment or stuck in traffic going to work. At a certain point, realizing you will be late, you let go, take a deep breath and say; "Oh well!", and settle into the situation. The more tense your breathing, the harder it is to release, let go of an experience.

Think of a time you were in pain...Breathing can be labored, shallow, quick...

Heightening every nerve in the body. Once you relax, starting with a single breath in and out, you gain control of the situation, or amount of discomfort experienced.

So, Okay, notice your breath, as it goes in and out. Become comfortable simply observing the natural rhythm of your breath.

Give yourself some time, some room to learn how to simply observe your breathing,

Without controlling it.

Now, observe your breathing without thinking about it. Simply allow your attention and focus to this particular moment.

All other things that you need to attend to will wait 5 minutes, sometimes 7 minutes, even if strategically timed, 20 minutes. To just notice breath without anything interfering, no things.

No reason thoughts can distract you from allowing this special time with simply yourself.

Believe it or not, you have just performed on act. You have also changed a habit you may not have been aware of; Thinking non-stop!

To give structure to breathing, practice taking a breath in through the nostrils while feeling the breath expand your belly, then at the bottom of your lungs, the middle and finally at the top of your lungs. Hold it for a moment, then release through the mouth, blowing. Again, practice.

Balance filling these sections. Pushing out the belly a little, as though air is filling this space gives room to fill your lungs more completely.

It moves stale air out also allowing for more absorption of

oxygen, feeding the entire body. Clearing the mind. Without air we cannot live, it is a nutrient. The brain needs this vital source.

When the brain is happy and satisfied, you are comfortable and have a sensation of well being.

Combine the above exercise with counting slowly up to 7 as you draw in a breath through your nostrils, pushing the belly out to fill your lungs systematically. Hold your breath to a count of 4, then release from the mouth on the count of 7.

You may increase the pause to 7 once you have practiced and mastered breathing.

Do this at first 3-5 times.

Notice how you feel or how your day goes afterwards. You may begin to find things that upset you may not be so important, or a solution comes to mind as to how to change the situation, or dealing with challenges.

It is totally amazing on how a simple exercise can positively affect many levels of our lives. Many famous people would take a 'nap' during the day, or the phrase; "I'll sleep on it" comes from the recognition that dropping a problem or issue for a short time, essentially walking away from it, allows the brain, the mind to organize, often producing an answer to a problem or challenge once we relax.

This technique is very portable, it is with you everywhere you go! Takes moments yet yields so much.

Remember it.

Practice it.

You can only prosper from it.

"If you want to change your life, Do it Flamboyantly and start Immediately."

William James

Self Hypnosis

In the following pages you will learn techniques of self hypnosis. You will want to record the self-hypnosis "scripts" I shall supply you with. In order to be successful in conquering anxiety and panic attacks remember to use all the tools provided in this book. If 'just' hypnotherapy worked, and sometimes to be honest it does, but not for all. Sometimes the anxiety or panic attacks morph into other symptoms such as migraine headaches, IBS, colitis and a host of other issues! If not completely irradiated from both the subconscious levels by utilizing hypnosis which reprograms the habituation and the 'cognitive behavior training', how and 'when' you are thinking.

If 'just' CBT worked on its own that would be great, and again, sometimes it does, but not for all and often what occurs is a management of the symptoms, but you still experience attacks.

Remember: All anxiety is based in the future: whether it is two minutes, two hours, two days, two weeks... and your perception of the future. (where you and the 'future' meet and what you tell yourself you're experience is going to be).

So, it is the combination of hypnosis, cognitive training, the reset button and all tips in this book that will allow you to move on with your life.

Worrier to Warrior, Conquering Anxiety and Panic Attacks has companion MP3's and books. It includes:

Audio:

1. Worrier to Warrior Introduction.
2. Mind-Spa Ultimate Healing
3. Anxiety & Panic Relief
4. Confidence, Organization & Focus
5. Self Trust & Serenity

Books:

1. Did You Know...
A Message of Choice & Change
1. Words that Empower "Enough-ism" vol VI

A description of these programs will be at the end of this book outlining what each program provides and the content of the books.

Before each self-hypnosis session remember these general rules:

Any audio recording may only be used in a safe environment. Under no circumstances is a hypnosis session to be used while operating a vehicle or where your attention is required. Please turn off your phone and plan to be un-disturbed for about 40 minutes. Or you may choose to go to bed to it. You will want to make sure you have used the restroom as a full blad-der is not conducive to relaxation.

Please find a comfortable place to relax either in bed or a comfortable chair. Loosen any tight or restrictive clothing. Do not cross your ankles, so as not to restrict blood flow.

If at any time during your session you need to reposition yourself, please do so, it will improve the quality of your experience. Simply follow the instructions, allow yourself to become as relaxed as possible.

Introducing the Self-Hypnosis portion of your liberation

Your job as you use your recordings is to become as comfortable as humanly possible, such as when you prepare to sleep at night or whenever you enter the sleep state.

☞ Turn off your phone.

☞ Let others if necessary, know you are to be undisturbed for 30-45 minutes. Hang a sign on your door.

☞ Find a comfy recliner or your bed, have a light blanket nearby as your body temperature drops similar as when you sleep at night.

☞ Do not have anything in your mouth to prevent choking.

☞ Listen to the entire recording, do not listen to a part of it!

☞ You may want a pillow to place under your knees or neck.

☞ Empty your bladder.

☞ If you have any aches or pains or discomforts, do your best to negotiate these, during the induction/hypnotic process, it will relieve you of them, often permanently, especially if it is emotionally based.

☞ You will experience the hypnotic rhythm, so do not be concerned if you do not pay attention or hear everything, your subconscious mind will record all the helpful suggestions you wish to receive.

☞ Listen & follow the progressive relaxation, then allow your mind to travel wherever it wants to go.

☞ You will need to have headphones or ear-buds, .

☞ Make your space as quiet as possible, once you are using the recording, noises or sounds will not disturb you, however, it is important you take the time to create let us say, a sanctuary... Your sanctuary of healing and restoration.

☞ You will only use the recordings in a safe environment, such as in your home where you control the environment.

☞ NEVER listen to the recording while driving or engaged in any activity such as operating a backhoe.

☞ There is nothing you can do wrong as you are entering hypnosis. When listening to the hypnosis recording, simply follow the instructions and enjoy as you are now healing and correcting the anxiety issues from where it is emerging, your subconscious... but remember, your conscious, thinking mind is giving it instructions to feel anxious or panic. So, we tackle and conquer by this two pronged approach, correct your thinking and set your subconscious up for success.

Throughout this process, you will be training your mind. At the end of this process, you will be in control of your mind, not the other way around where you believe you are a slave or victim to its whims, or like there is something wrong with you and you just need to deal with it,

You are now learning and practicing to Master your mind instead of your mind mastering you.

☞ Listen to it sometime during the day, however, you may listen to it going to sleep. You may when you want a 'tune up', but for the purposes of this program, please use as instructed for correction of the anxiety/panic issues. Think of it like taking medication, like an antibiotic; you need to take the full course, even though you may be feeling better the third or fourth day in... otherwise you will create a super bug and need a stronger course of medication.

☞ Simply prepare your space as mentioned and follow the instructions, easy peasy. There is nothing you can do wrong. Will you still be thinking while you are being hypnotized? Yes. Hypnosis works with both the conscious and subconscious levels of mind activity. (thought ceases when you're worm food)

☞ You can enhance its effects by utilizing your five senses:

☞ Visualization/pretending or remembering what is being described. I will describe at some point a lake on a warm day. If you use your imagination to see the lake, feel the warm breeze, the warmth of the sun on your skin, the taste in the air, hear the birds chirping in the background, this will enhance your experience greatly.

☞ Listen to Hypnosis Script #1 Mind-Spa once for two days/nights, wait four to seven days and then listen to it again. More is not always better. Your psyche needs time to process information.

Now, many people experience results or cessation of symptoms from the first listening of Script #1, most people experience results after the second session.

☞ After listening to #1 Mind-Spa, you will notice you feel a lot calmer, more in control.

☞ Remember your reset button technique breathing exercise, a minimum of twice a day. Pay attention if you are thinking about the future. If nothing needs your immediate attention, don't concern yourself, stay present in the present, where your power exists. Most people, after listening the first time will never have a full blown panic attack again, you might get to the edge, but not go over. Use the reset button technique, the tepid water, mint and stating to yourself that you are safe, and this will pass in a few moments.

☞ Remember, the cognitive part, watching and changing what and when you are thinking about at the conscious level, and the hypnotherapy resetting your fight/flight/freeze response at the subconscious level, you will be good to go.

☞ Once you have listened to Script #1 Mind-Spa twice, you ought to be primarily symptom free. If this is true for you, move on to the other Scripts. Always use the recordings once for two days then four to seven days apart... In my office I see clients every 4-10 days apart, so I split the difference and see them 7 days apart.

☞ If for whatever reason you cannot listen four days apart, it can be within ten days... no worries.

☞ As you are recording speak slowly and clearly, pace yourself. In the Scripts you will see "..." this is to remind you to pace...pace...pause, etc.

Important Note:

Once you correct the anxiety and/or panic attacks, and may be on medications, by no means stop taking a medication that is not an "as needed." If you are on a daily dose, you must consult your healthcare provider and discuss your desires to safely discontinue use, there are many meds that need to be dosed down, and if not done correctly can cause you harm.

Progressive Relaxation

This exercise requires setting aside some time, at least 20-45 minutes to begin with. As you become proficient, a few minutes, even the thought of relaxing will allow you to completely enter a place of comfort physically, mentally and throughout your entire being.

However, exercise is exercise, and takes a little dedication and practice. Once you add a new routine to your life, after a while, it becomes second nature. Usually 21 days or three weeks.

Begin by finding a comfortable position either lying down or in a comfy chair. Turn off your phone or on a silent setting, allow voice mail to catch the call, and let it be okay. Dedicate this time solely to yourself, choose to avoid any distractions. Decide this is a gift to yourself, uninterrupted.

Loosen any tight clothing, and allow yourself to shift around until your body becomes so relaxed you become still. There is no wrong way to do this exercise. It is a learned skill. Focus your attention to your breath for a moment. Breathe in slowly and deliberately through the nostrils if comfortable, pause, and release through the mouth. Do this 3-5 times.

Close your eyes to prevent any environmental distractions. Move your attention and imagination to your feet, the toes. Pick one toe, the large one on either foot and move it up and down. Then relax it. Relax every tissue, tendon and muscle. Move your attention to the next toe, flex it if you want, or pretend your breath is going into it and as the breath releases, it releases any tension, stress or strain in this toe, and so on...
Move your attention to the balls of the foot, into the heel and ankle. Flex the heel and ankle, noticing the difference of tension and release, then moving up into the calf then knee, relaxing every tendon, every muscle, every tissue, down to the cellular level. Be aware of any pressure and pretend to breathe into it or flex it, then let it go.

Move along the body up to the thigh and hip, along the side of your belly into the ribcage. Tell these portions of your body to relax, be at ease.

Remind yourself if necessary that you do not need to be anywhere but here. Focus all of your thought and attention on letting go of physical stress, tension and frustration. Be patient with yourself, it may be the first time learning how to relax. It may feel weird.

Your breathing has naturally slowed and is rhythmic and paced. Bring your attention to the shoulder and neck. Move down the upper arm, elbow, wrist and down through each finger. Imagine tension draining out of your finger-tips like a faucet opened, releasing every stress, strain and thought. Use your imagination to see, feel or hear the sensation of stress, strain, physical discomfort draining from your entire body, with the rhythm of your breathing. Imagine as you inhale the breath is circulating through-out your entire body, soaking up any aches, pains, any thoughts that are not focused upon simply relaxing. As you exhale allow this to drain from your fingertips. Move attention again to the neck and up along the side of the jaw. Open and close your jaw if you observe any tension here, then into the cheek and eye. Relax your head moving across to the other side, down to the ear and down the back. Focus your attention to the upper neck, feel the ver-tebrae moving along the spine, across the shoulder blades, feeling them part slightly, releasing tension, stress and strain.

Every muscle, every tendon, every tissue at ease and com-fortable. Move down to the center of your back, the sides and into the lower portion, near the hips. Breathe into these areas, instruct it to relax and release, as though you are preparing to sleep.

At this moment, you may notice the difference in the sides of your body, one side tense, the other utterly relaxed. You may move your attentions to the large toe on the opposite foot, and follow the same route up and through this side of your body, but usually the body will take the cue and relax totally.

Once this is achieved, any suggestions you want to give will take hold. The body at this state is in balance. The body naturally repairs damage at this level and will leave you with a sense of well being. Your thoughts and tensions held in the muscles, tendons and tissues releases and a clearing, a cleansing occurs, on a physical and psychological level.

You may want to begin with the following suggestions:

"Every day in every way I am better and better. I am stronger, calmer, confident, wiser, peaceful, patient with myself and others, healthier in mind, in body, in spirit, in all way, in every way. So it is."

When you are finished, instruct yourself that in a few moments you shall open your eyes feeling fully awake, alert and refreshed, in mind, in body and in all ways. If you are going to sleep instruct yourself that you will receive the best nights sleep you've had in a long time and that you will awaken refreshed in mind and body alike, in all ways, in every way.

You may want to record this exercise on a your phone or CD and pop it in a player or simply follow the guidance.

The state of relaxation is the point.

It is the spacious present desired.

With practice comes mastery. With mastery comes control.

It is always wise to remember that most of us are doing the best we can with what we know at any given moment. One of the most amazing blessings in and of life is time, choice, change...

At any given moment we can choose to make a new choice!

Introduction
Script #1: Mind-Spa

The Mind-Spa session is specifically designed to release, and transmutes old, inhibitive energies, beliefs, past impressions in perceptions. We sometimes unknowingly hold on to past emotional issues in our energy fields, within the subconscious as well as in the body. Do you have aches or pains that do not appear to have any known origin?

Are you doing your utmost best to create changes, but find little or limited success? Are your energies low, like you are suffering from an exhaustion, yet do not feel you are expending that much energy to warrant feeling worn down...What about your weight, does it seem to have a mind of its own, fluctuating beyond your best efforts. Do you find yourself procrastinating, putting things off or simply not wanting to deal with issues, situations in your life, even though you know better?

If you have some or all of these issues, you are carrying around emotional debris, emotional baggage.

I like to describe it like this: We all have a receptacle, or garbage can within our home. Once it fills up, we then take the garbage out to a larger trash can to be taken away. Sometimes, after we have sorted through issues in our lives, and we have moved beyond them, we still seem haunted by having challenges in manifesting our decisions. This is because somehow you 'forgot' to take out the trash in the house for it to be taken away. Once you experience the Mind-Spa Session, you will have immediate relief; feel physically lighter, as though a heavy burden has been lifted off of your body, your being. You will experience fresh energy, creative vitality and new ideas to align you with your highest good.

If you are having financial, career issues. new avenues open up. If you are having issues with communications with loved ones, friends, co-workers or your staff, you will find and discover new in-roads and ability to effectively communicate what you want from others, and allow others to hear your needs.

If you are experiencing issues with sleep, organization and focus these as well begin to shift, and you find you are balanced in body, mind and energy/spirit. These are some of the wonderful benefits you will achieve and experience.

Mind-Spa has two portions: Script #1 for the relief and remission of anxiety/panic and the above mentioned. Script #2 are affirmations to correctly state your intentions that creates and promotes self confidence, self esteem, self awareness and self sufficiency.

If you are taking medications: Once you feel the shift in your life, and the elimination of anxiety/panic attacks, this is now the time to speak to your doc or therapist prescribing medications to mitigate the symptoms you may like to discontinue. Under no circumstances, unless they are an 'as needed' type med, are you to do this on your own. Trust me on this point it can be harmful even dangerous.

Hypnosis Session Script #1

Mind-Spa

Breathe in slowly and deeply through your nose, close your eyes, merely to block out any distractions and exhale completely through your mouth and begin to relax...just think about relaxing and releasing every muscle in your body from the top of your head to the tips of your toes... and begin to notice how very comfortable your body is beginning to feel...just let go...inhale and exhale...notice the rhythm of your breathing and relax your breathing for a moment...be aware of normal sounds around you... you may hear people walking or talking beyond this room... you may perhaps even hear the sounds of traffic...these sounds are unimportant...these sound will cause you relax deeper knowing you are absolutely safe and secure in this time this place and this moment...

...whatever you hear from now on will only help to relax you...

and as you exhale...release any tension...any stress from any part of your body, mind and thought...just let that stress go...just feel any thoughts rushing through your mind...feel them begin to wind down, wind down, wind down, you may even imagine the thoughts in your mind as items on a table in front of you, filling it to its edges and you can imagine taking your arm and pushing these items to the side, creating a space...these thoughts are still there if you need them..

and now... relax...and begin with releasing all the muscles in your face relax...especially your jaw...let your teeth part just a little bit and release this area...this is a place where tension and stress gather so be sure and release your jaw and feel that relaxation go into your temples and relax the muscles in your temples, and as you think about relaxing these muscles they will relax...

...feel them relax and as you relax you'll be able to just drift and float into a deeper and deeper level of total total comfort...

...now let go of all the muscles in your forehead relax...feel those muscles smooth, smooth and relaxed...and relax your eyes...just imagine your eyelids feeling so comfortable...so heavy...so relaxed...

...and now let go of all the muscles in the back of your neck and shoulders relax...feel a heavy, heavy weight being lifted off your shoulders and you feel relieved...lighter and more at ease...and all the muscles in the back of your neck and shoulders release...and that soothing relaxation go down your back...down, down, down...to the lower part of your back...and those muscles let go and with every breath you inhale... just feel your body drifting...floating, down deeper, down deeper, down deeper...into total,

.ultimate relaxation.....let your muscles go...releasing more and more...let all the muscles in your shoulders, running down your arms to your fingertips...relax...

...and let your arms feel so heavy, so comfortable...

...and now you inhale once again and relax your chest muscles...and as you exhale...feel your stomach muscles relax...as you exhale, relax all the muscles in your stomach...let them go...and all the muscles in your legs, feel them relax...and all the muscles in your legs...so completely relaxed right to the tips of your toes...

...notice how very comfortable your body feels...just drifting and floating....deeper, deeper, relaxed...

...as you are relaxing deeper and even deeper...imagine a beautiful descending staircase...there are 10 steps and the 10 steps lead you to a special and peaceful and beautiful place...in a moment you can begin to imagine taking a safe and gentle and easy step down, down,...on the staircase...leading you to a very private peaceful...a very special place for you...you can imagine it to be any place you choose...perhaps you would enjoy a beach or ocean with clean, fresh air...or the mountains with a stream...any place is perfectly fine.....in a moment you can imagine taking the steps down and as you take each step...feel your body relax and release more and more...feel it just drift down, down with each step...

....and relax even deeper 10...relax even deeper...9 all concerns and worries lifting off and away from you...8 feeling freer and lighter...7 feeling relieved...6 relaxing deeper now...5 almost there...4 calm and free of stress...3 absolute comfort...2 experiencing joy and....1...deeper, deeper... relaxed...

...and now imagine a peaceful and special place...you can imagine this place and perhaps even feel it...you are in a special place...you are alone and there is no one around to disturb you...

...this is the most peaceful place in the world for you... imagine yourself there and feel a sense of peace flow through you and a sense of well being... and enjoy these positive feelings and keep them with you long after this session is completed...for the rest of this day and evening...tomorrow...allow these positive feelings to grow stronger and stronger...feeling at peace with a sense of well being...and each and every time that you choose to do this type of relaxation...you will be able to relax deeper and deeper... regardless of any stress and tension that may surround your life...you may now remain more at peace...more calm...more relaxed...and allow the tension and stresses to bounce off and away from you...just bounce off and away from you...and these positive feelings will stay with you and grow stronger and stronger throughout the day as you continue to relax deeper and deeper.

(Deepening the trance) You may use this deepening script when you practice the Reset Button Technique to enhance your sense of physical, emotional and psychological comfort.

...take time now to finally get in touch with yourself...to feel the wonderful, soothing calm...that is moving and flowing through your body...as you allow your mind to travel wherever it wants to go...

now, you may breathe healing throughout your body, releasing any remaining tension...imagining that you are inhaling colors of rainbows reds and oranges of warming... relaxing colors of throughout yourself...inhaling rainbows of yellows throughout your entire body...and exhaling any disturbances or imbalances...and again, inhaling beautiful warming colors of greens and blues and purple violet... and exhaling any imbalances or discomforts...and one more time...inhaling rainbows of warming, relaxing colors silver and gold...throughout your body...and exhaling into perfect, peaceful healing, perfect health in body and mind alike..

...you may continue to breathe at your own pace...as slowly and as deeply as is comfortable for you...imagining the air is breathing for you...and noticing that as the air enters your body...like a soothing ray of sunshine... warming and relaxing you...as you allow yourself...to drift and float...further and further into total....peaceful, blissful relaxation...

(To enhance hypnosis utilize any of your five senses to see, feel, hear, taste, smell where you imagine yourself to be in your visualizations)

..Imagine now you are now walking along a beach barefoot...Its late in the afternoon...the sun has not yet begun to set but it is getting low on the horizon...

...a soft gentle breeze blows caressing your skin, it feels so so good...the gentle breeze is welcoming you and you notice you see the vast sea...

The sun is a golden blazing yellow, the sky a brilliant blue, the sand a dazzling glistening white in the sunlight

...Feel the soft sand beneath your feet...

...Taste and smell the salt in the air...

...Hear the beating of the waves, the rhythmic lapping to and fro, back n forth of the water kissing the shore...

...Hear the far off cry of a distant seagull as you continue to walk...

...Suddenly you come to a sand dune, a mound of pure white sand...You sit down on its crest and look out to sea...

...The sea is like a mirror of silver reflecting the suns rays, a mass of pure pure white light, and you are gazing intently into this light...

...As you continue to stare at the suns reflection off the water, you begin to see flecks of violet, darting spots of purple intermingled with the silver...

...Everywhere there is silver and violet...

...There is violet along the horizon line... a violet halo around the flowers...

...Now the sun is beginning to set...

...With each movement, with each motion of the sun into the sea you become deeper and deeper relaxed ......You are engulfed in a deep purple twighlight, a velvety blue haze...

...The sun is just about to set...

...You look up into the sky and watch large puffy clouds...

...Around the edges of the clouds are the colors of the set-ting sun...

...Notice how softly the colors shift from crimson to or-ange... As you watch the shifting colors in the sky deep within the clouds notice how your feelings also shift from relaxed to calm to peaceful......Watch the clouds as they move and grow......Move and become distant......Their shapes shift easily and effortlessly, quietly yet effec-tively......Just like your feelings change, grow and release, moving far off into the distance thoughts, feelings and pain or discomforts that no longer reflect who you are......You are now a confident person...

...Any need to punish yourself will simply go away from you...as a matter of fact... It will go so far and so distant until it will be just like floating on a cloud...Just like floating into the distance...

...Just like floating so far away and so distant until you can hardly see it at all... (wait 10 seconds)

...Now focus on one of the clouds in the beautiful sky still alight with colors of soft blues and hues of purple-violet ...Focus on one of the large towering clouds for a moment...Just watch the cloud floating into the distance...

...Floating so far and so distant until it becomes so small and so insignificant that you can hardly notice it at all...

Now The sky has darkened with night and twinkling stars...You look up into the night sky...It is a brilliant starry night...

...The beating of the waves, the smell and taste of the salt, the sea, the sky......You feel yourself carried upward and outward into space, one with the universe (repeat x3 wait 15 seconds)

...This is your special place, you are calm, free and at peace...At complete peace......You may visit your special place any time you take a slow, deep breath......Instantly a slow, deep breath will bring you to your special place of calmness, all fear, anxiety and discomfort just melt away, melt off and away...

...Fear and discomfort or anxiety just simply dissolve flow-ing away...You experience all situations now comfortably, confidently...You are in control in all environments ...

...Now, you may visualize all the things that you wish to accomplish...Or that you wish to have happen...

See your life occurring exactly how you want it to occur, now... (wait 10 seconds)

...now mentally step into this perfect picture...that you have created in your mind Knowing that it will soon be your reality...

...now focus on a happy, healthy, successful image of your-self, in a moment you slowly return to a normal plane of awareness...that's right, coming back slowly counting up from one to 10... to the here and now...

...all suggestion are permanently seated deep within your subconscious mind to help you automatically in every situation and in every circumstance in which you find yourself whether alone or with others....returning to full waking consciousness, feeling refreshed as though you had a long rest...you will bring back all feelings of safety, your strength emotionally and physically continues to grow and... any stress during the day shall melt off and away from you as you operate from a center of balance and self-confidence...you are strong you are confident you are safe in all ways every way...in mind and body alike, in spirit...You may choose to return to the present, the here and now alert and refreshed in three minutes or you may chose to go to sleep at this moment...

For sleep:.. enjoy the feeling of your body melting, melting, melting into the surface beneath you....feel yourself drift-ing deeper into peaceful...pleasant feelings of comfort and pleasure...notice you feel warm and tired.. as you become aware of these feelings you may allow yourself to drift off into your own little world...into you own comfortable level of peaceful sleep, sleep.

Coming up

Beginning to come back now...1...coming back to this time this place and this moment refreshed and confident... tonight you shall have the best nights sleep you've had in a long time...and every night that follows from this day forward you allow yourself to completely rest and sleep when you lay down for the evening...

...You now find it easy and effortless to let go of thoughts of the day and plans for tomorrow when you lay dawn at night to rest to sleep...you will sleep deeply and soundly receiving that amount of rest necessary to refresh and re-store and revitalize you...

2 slowly returning to this time this place restored in mind and body alike the feelings of relaxation and tranquility will remain with you...

3 safely, comfortably, returning to the present moment feeling a great deal of pride and achievement and accomplished and satisfaction of your growing abilities ...

4 to 5 coming back comfortably to full waking consciousness feeling happy and satisfied, satisfied of your continued progress and growth satisfied your body is healing and stronger, healthier each and every day...

...you are confident and comfortable in all situations...

...you are comfortable and in control in all environments...

...you eat balanced healthful meals in the correct proportions and feel satisfied ...

6 back now to this time and place feeling refreshed and energetic feeling invigorated and ready...

7 feeling free and light all excess weight, burdens has lifted off and away from you any and all excess weight has lifted off and away you now have clear focus a can begin to notice your daily life becomes organized and focused...

8 become aware of your body, as your circulation, breathing, body temperature return to normal your mind back to full alertness ...

9 take in a deep cleansing breath, open your eyes you are in full control of your mind and body to this time this place this moment fully refreshed and energized to accomplish the rest of your day...

and 10 completely back, take another deep breath feeling free and light and energized, you are the master of your mind, ruler of your body.

Hypnosis Script #2

Affirmations

Use Hypnosis Script #1, Mind-Spa up to "deepening trace" or "Coming Up." then add the following:

...I have the courage, will to do all the things I want to do

I now allow myself to succeed with ease

I now choose to be totally fulfilled personally and professionally, confidently

Every day in every way I am stronger and stronger

Every day I am calmer and confident

Every day I am patient with myself and others

Every day in every way I am healthier in mind, body, spirit

I view barriers as opportunities to reassess and open

I am capable of doing anything I set my mind/decision to

My capacities and abilities are endless, my wisdom is limitless

I clearly see myself succeeding at everything I choose to do

I am relaxed and focused on my goals and desires

I am creating my own vibrant health, satisfaction and successes with my thoughts, decisions and actions

I now set goals for myself each day

I make time to relax and appreciate myself each day

I now release any beliefs that block my success and happiness

I am powerful...my highest purpose is becoming clear to me now...I will achieve my highest good in life easily

I have and develop all the strength and courage to do all the things I want to do and achieve in an easy flow

I am more creatively inspired each day

I have an amazing ability to be spontaneous and flexible

I am directing my subconscious mind to focus on the things that I have chosen to accomplish and satisfy

I now direct my subconscious mind to reveal to me talents, strengths, courage and creativity, lying dormant, so that I may utilize these talents and strengths, now or in it's own timing

My subconscious mind works elegantly for me, revealing the perfect solutions to questions and challenges

I communicate my needs to others in a clear and effective way that encourages others to respond to my needs

It is easy for me to organize and prioritize to get my work done without hesitation or doubt

I accept challenges knowing that I will feel great and satisfied when my challenges are solved

I am removing and releasing all obstacles from my life

The gifts and rewards from all I do will expand

I possess everything that I need to know in my subconscious mind to become a total success

I rely on myself for happiness, strength and courage

I am a planner and a doer

I am fearless being who I am, being me, uniquely

Energy flows, flows easily, freely through my body

My creativity is always flowing and growing

I am courageous, confident, smart and attractive

I do everything with love, joy, passion and laughter

My passions and interests in life grow stronger and stronger

I feel safe in the flow of my life

I am more and more content

I am patient and kind with myself

I feel free free free to express me

I am healthy in mind, body in all ways in every way

So it is

You may use either the "Coming Up" script or the "Sleep" script from Hypnosis Script #1

Introduction: Script #3
Anxiety & Panic Relief

If after the second use of Script #1, Mind-Spa session you are still experiencing symptoms, use this recording. Gain control of Anxiety and Panic Attacks. For optimal results, please use headphones. Learn how to relax and release bodily tension. Learn how to control your breath and shut down the rush of adrenaline (Fight or Flight or Freeze Response) Learn to eliminate a panic attack in less than three minutes. Learn to correct permanently, anxiety and panic attacks. You inadvertently created it, you can un-create it.

☞ You will only use this recording in a safe place, NEVER while driving or as background or subliminally. * Tips: To leach the adrenaline from your body sip room temperature water, takes about 3-7 minutes. To relax your stomach and discomfort drink Mint tea, take a mint, such as Altoids. An Apple also works for calming the stomach and stimulating appetite. Do the Reset Button Technique 3-5 times.

To release tension, relax your jaw, drop your shoulders and relax your belly. Now take in a deep breath, pause for a second or two, then exhale, blowing the air out of your mouth like you are blowing soap bubbles... do this very slowly. Continue 5-10 times, paying attention to your shoulders remaining in a relaxed position. To stop rapid thoughts, Stop thinking about the future and how you are feeling, all anxiety is based on your thoughts of the future. Anchor yourself in the Present moment. Change your location, take a walk, write an email, etc. Get out of your head and into your environment.

Hypnosis Script #3

General Relaxation & Deepening with Stairs &

3 min Anxiety and Panic Attack Release

Slowly draw in 3 deep breaths...

With each breath, every inhalation allow all thoughts of the day of yesterday and later release, releasing with each and every exhalation...Inhaling relaxation, with each breath...Allowing your own comfort/ease/relaxation to occur... ..allowing all tension all stress all strain release like knots loosening... as you exhale...

...allowing, yes any and all frustration to release through each exhalation...letting go into total comfort & ease knowing you are safe and secure in this time this place this moment...

...allow your body to sink into peace and profound comfort...as your muscles, the tendons and tissues every cell nerve and fiber in your body release all tension, stress, all strain easily and effortlessly... easily and effortlessly....now becoming aware... noticing with each and every inhalation you draw in relaxation, comfort and ease...as you exhale, letting go of physical tension, letting go easily and effortlessly...and with each breath you are deeper and deeper relaxed...

filling you with comfort, peace and absolute balance... absolute balance...each and every exhalation releasing, releasing, simply letting go of tension and stress no longer necessary...

...your body is becoming so very comfortable, so so comfortable is feels like a heavy heavy weight has been lifted, lifted, away...feeling a calm in mind, in body, in all ways...

...feeling calm feeling relaxed and enjoying where you are

...and with each inhalation and exhalation going deeper and deeper relaxed and peaceful, feeling strong in mind and body, in all ways, feeling strong in mind and body alike, in all ways, all ways...

...now...imagine within the confines of your inner mind a soothing ray of golden sunshine, a warm shower of relaxation that penetrates every muscle, every tendon, every tissue, a warm shower of relaxation releasing all stress, all strain...

...feeling that shower like a warm blanket, imagine and experience the warmth moving down, down from your head your face, the warm shower dissolving, soothing all tension from the forehead, eyebrows, feel your lips slightly part, the warmth moving through your jaw, become aware of any tension in the jaw and release it...your swallow comfortable and easy as that warmth moves down, deeper and even deeper into the neck and shoulders arms and hands...out through the finger tips...feeling that golden shower of relaxation washing away all stress all strain from body and mind alike...a golden shower of relaxation moving down through the chest, belly and back...

becoming even more and more comfortable, safe and secure...

...that shower of relaxation moves down, down through the hips and thighs each and every muscle melting, melting into perfect comfort...

...moving down deeper now, deeper into the knees, that warmth relaxing so comfortable so pleasant...at ease now in mind and body alike, in all ways, in every way...

...feel that golden shower of relaxation moving down the lower legs and ankles, into the feet... through the tips of the toes... easily and effortlessly that golden shower dissolves washes all tension, stress strain away, away, completely away as though its going down a drain..

...as you travel into deep relaxation, so calm and safe, safe in mind in body in all ways so calm and safe, a shield of peacefulness of security surround and hold you...

...hold you as though strong arms held you close protecting you... being held safe, secure and strong as you travel, you are held by strong protective arms...tenderly as a shield ...this shield protects you in mind, protecting you in body in all ways, in every way...

...this shield is always here protecting you...simply draw in an inhalation...

... you can feel this shield surrounding you protecting you from fear, from anxiety no fear can get through that shield...

if you ever feel you are losing control you always have the tools to regain it...you stop, breath deeply, relax and you feel that shield around you, the shield protects you from fear, protects you from anxiety no fear or anxiety can get through that shield...

...the fear just melts away, melts away when it reaches the shield, the anxiety just dissolves and flows away, dis-solves and flows off and away, off and away from you...going down a drain...

...imagine yourself in control in all situations, being in control of all the parts of your daily routine... If you ever feel you are losing control you always have the tools to re-gain it. You stop, breathe deeply, relax and you feel that shield around you, the shield that protects you from fear... protects you from anxiety...no fear, no anxiety can get through that shield...the fear just melts away when it reaches the shield, the anxiety just dissolves and flows away, just dissolves and flows away off and away, going down a drain...you are so relaxed and calm...

now imagine yourself in a car, feeling calm, feeling relaxed and enjoying where you are, and looking forward to
traveling... now Feel your hands comfortably wrapped
around the wheel...

...You feel comfortable and confident, comfortable and confident comfortable and confident, in control...The car is
like a shield, protecting you strong and confident surrounding you protectively, gently...and now Become
aware...

...You are comfortable and confident in all situations...

...You are comfortable and confident in all environments...

...You are comfortable and confident within your very own
skin...

...You are comfortable and confident in all places, spaces
& rooms, large, small, every place, space room has a door,
an entrance...

Every room must be entered through a door...All environments are open or enclosed...

All environments must be entered through a door...And
Easily and effortlessly you pass through doors...You are in
control in all situations...Your are comfortable and confident...now become aware... you now enter all situations
at complete ease...Feel how peaceful and relaxed you are.

(Deepener, you may also use this with any of the scripts or breathing techniques or Reset Button)

Now imagine, pretend, see....in front of you stairs descending...

...There are 10 steps leading to a special private place of peace and possibility...

..In a moment count each step as you slowly go down... With each step your relaxation shall increase...

10, 100,1000 x's...

...In a moment, each step down you will become deeper relaxed...With each step your body becomes lighter...

Each step light and free...Each step all cares and worries simply release...Leaving all burdens and worries behind...

...Now Feel your feet upon the stairs...Assured, confident and joyful...Confident you will have a wonderful time, a pleasantly delightful time as you travel to a private place just beyond the bottom of the stairs...

10 feel yourself begin to descend...feel your body relax even deeper now

9.....Feeling light free and at complete ease...leaving now all concerns and worries behind

8 deeper relaxed now, the deeper relaxed you become the

more confident you feel the more confident you feel the deeper relaxed you are...

and 7 feeling even freer and lighter all weight all burdens dissolving/floating away at total ease as you allow yourself to go even deeper now...

...you are balanced in body, mind and spirit...each step confidence soars to new heights...

...and 6 so comfortable and centered...feelings of wellbeing and satisfaction deepens...

...each step down feeling lighter and freer...relaxed and alive...personal satisfaction/strength surrounds and fills you with joy and peace...

and the deeper you relax the stronger your personal satisfaction/strength ...the deeper your satisfaction/strength the more relaxed you become...

...and 5 you are nearing the bottom of the stairs, noticing how calm and peaceful you are...

4 you feel as though you are light as a feather...excited as you move forward...confident with each and every step...

3 these feelings of ease of personal satisfaction/strength and confidence shall be yours all the days of your life,

2 almost there, excited as you enter private place of peace and possibilities

and 1, you have arrived...you are in a private place...

...let yourself drift deeper and deeper...deeper and deeper, drifting and drowsy, drowsy and drifting...drifting down, down into total relaxation...drifting deeper and deeper... you are safe ...

...you are aware now that symptoms of anxiety are your body's nature fight flight freeze response...they are natural and harmless...they are unimportant... unimpertant... and you are losing your fear of the symptoms/expressions of anxiety...you are unafraid of the symptoms of anxiety... they are your body's natural fight flight freeze response... you accept the harmless symptoms of anxiety...you remind yourself you are medically safe...right now you remind yourself of what your symptoms mean and why you are medically safe...(pause)...

whatever your symptoms,...you know they are unimportant and that you are medically safe...the symptoms are natural...you are losing the fear of the symptoms of anxiety...you are becoming stronger...more confident...more self assured...you are in control of the fears and anxieties...

...you can relax your body whenever you feel fear or panic...you can breath deeply, deeply...the air will push deep into your abdomen...deep down into your belly...

...take a deep breath into your belly...and let go...exhale that old air...you can take slow, deep breaths to regulate

your breathing...deep breaths into your belly, slowly letting go...whenever you feel anxious you can begin taking
slow deep breaths into your abdomen...

...take another deep breath to remind to remind yourself
that you can regulate your breathing...you will breathe
slowly, deeply, if ever you feel anxious...you can reset
your whole body...when you are anxious you can check
your body for tension...you will check the shoulders and
neck, letting the shoulders droop and relax...you will
check the jaw, letting the jaw hang loosely, loosely...you
will check the forehead, letting it become smooth, smooth
and relaxed...you will check the abdomen, letting each
deep breath relax your stomach...each deep breath relaxing the stomach more and more deeply...you can relax any
part of the body that feels tension...when you are anxious...you will check and relax any tension area in the
body...you know you are in charge...you have the tools
and knowledge to let go of all anxiety and fear...

...you know the truth now...that panic passes quickly
when you stop the anxious thoughts...panic passes
quickly...it passes in less than 3 minutes...when you
empty the mind of anxious thoughts...you can wait it out
and soon...very soon it will be over...when you are feeling
anxiety and panic and you can stop the anxious thoughts,
stop the thoughts of danger ...inside your mind you will
shout "stop!" to the anxious thoughts...

knowing the panic will passes in less than 3 min...you can shout "stop!" inside your mind to cease the anxious thoughts...panic passes quickly, its over, over, over...panic passes and its over when you stop the anxious thoughts... you can wait it out and soon the panic will be over...you are in charge...you have the ability to release all panic and anxious thoughts...

...imagine the anxiety as a picture hanging in a museum... perhaps a picture of war or strife or anguish...see the picture on the wall of the museum...you are moving past the picture...floating past the picture...you are almost past the picture...and now it disappears from sight...the anxiety passes like the picture out of sight, out of sight...you can accept any emotion because you float past, float past, float past until it is gone out of sight...you accept and float past your feelings...

...now you have new responses to your old anxious thoughts...you no longer frighten yourself with the catastrophic fears...you are letting go of the old fear, the old anxiety...letting go, letting go, letting go...of the old fears...right now you can remind yourself of your new responses to the old anxious thoughts...(pause)

...whenever you are aware of the old anxious thoughts, you know now that you can stop them...those thoughts are fading, fading, fading...see them fading like a light going out in the distance...you have new responses to the old anxious thought you know you can accept any feeling in your body...you can accept any emotion...you accept without running from your feelings and emotions...you accept without running...you float past anxiety and panic...knowing it is a brief time and in a short while you feel so much better...you float past without fighting...you know now that your feelings are transient and passing...they are passing, passing (like clouds in the sky) and soon will be gone...your feelings, no matter how uncomfortable pass and are gone...they are gone...the anxiety or panic soon will be gone......you accept and float past your feelings

you are becoming stronger and stronger...more and more confident...you are stronger and more confident because you accept and let feelings pass...you embrace your feelings...both painful and pleasurable...because they pass and soon are gone...you have nothing to fear because you accept your feelings...you are hopeful and confident...you are able now to cope with your feelings...you can relax and cope...see yourself walking tall and straight...see and feel the strength in your step...you accept the future without worry because you can cope with panic and anxiety...you can cope and float past the panic...in under three minutes the panic will be over if you relax and take slow deep breaths... you empty your mind of anxious thoughts...in under three minutes...any panic will be over if you float past, letting go of anxious thoughts...

...and now you will be able to enter any situation where you once felt stressed...you can enter because you accept your feelings...you can cope with your feelings...you go wherever you want and you do whatever you want because you are confident in your ability to cope...you know now that you can enter any situation and remember your coping skills...you have new abilities to cope and you feel a growing confidence in your abilities to cope... because you can float past the fear...letting go, letting go, letting go...feeling so strong...so confident...you are in charge... you are able to cope with any stressful situations...you feel very relaxed...very peaceful...and in a few moments you will come back to full conscious awareness feeling stronger and more positive...feeling confident and strong...

(You may end here and proceed to "Coming Up" or continue with remaining script on following pages.

You may want to create a separate recording of the Companion induction to follow at a different time. If you choose to do this, use the general relaxation session, the deepener then skip forward to Companion. It is best to give your self a few days between self-hypnosis session to allow the information to absorb, assimilate, process and then be utilized by the subconscious.)

...now allow yourself to drift down deeper, deeper,...now just imagine that some time has passed, a day or two, perhaps a week or a month...see yourself in the near future... imagine that you have made tremendous progress...you have let go of the old fears...old anxieties....you now have new coping skills...new tools that give you control over the anxieties and stresses... each day you grow stronger... more confident...more self assured....you can cope with any situation regardless of how stressful...you have practiced your new techniques and have stopped panic attacks before they had a chance to start...many of the old fears are far behind you and are fading more and more each day...this image of the future is your new blueprint... bring it to the present moment and it will begin to manifest itself and grow stronger and stronger each day...

...Now, imagine for a moment that you have just stopped a panic attack by using your new skills...you breathe easy... you feel steady...your chest and stomach are calm...you have succeeded...you have accomplished your goal...you have won...you have control...the feeling is wonderful... you feel proud of yourself...you feel a great sense of confidence...you know that you can do it...imagine a smile on your face...see yourself standing tall...you enjoy life now without all the old fears...they are just old baggage from the past...you have let them go...you are able to cope with any situation regardless of how stressful they may be... you float through them...you just float through them...let them go...let them fade, fade, fade away...you have strength...confidence...you are in charge of your life...now conclude your imagery by seeing yourself in your special place and reflect on all of your new and powerful feelings of confidence...trusting trusting yourself to cope with any situation...and liking who you are...just enjoy these positive feelings for a few more minutes.

...In a few moments count from 1 to 5...when you reach the number 5 you will be fully alert, awake and totally refreshed in mind and body alike...the feelings of relaxation and tranquility will remain with you...any stress or tension shall melt off and away from you as you are now centered...focused and confident...all suggestions are seated deep within your subconscious mind to help you automatically in every situation and in every circumstance in which you find yourself...whether alone or with others... you are now comfortable and confident in all environments...you are now comfortable and confident in all situations...you are now comfortable and confident within your very own skin... you communicate well with those around you and you communicate in a way that makes others want to respond to your needs...

Coming Up:

1 Beginning to come up to full alertness... you are mentally alert...emotionally stable and physically stronger and stronger...

1 to 2...your mind is clear...your heart is full...your soul is free ...your body heals and you are happy...

2 to 3...you will have the best nights sleep tonight...and your sleep will continue to improve...awakening in the morning refreshed...restored...and full of creative energy motivation with fresh ideas...you are always moving in the direction of your optimal health and happiness...all systems in your body function perfectly...

3 to 4...take a deep breath as you become aware of your body press upon the bed (chair)...your breathing, body temperature and heart rate are returning to normal... from 4 to 5 take another deep breath...you are now back to a normal plane of awareness...fully alert and in full control of your mind, in full control of your body... remembering, you are the master of your mind and ruler of your body...yes.

> **TIP:**
>
> Imagine a ceiling fan spinning. Now flip the switch to turn it off. Watch as it slows down steadily. After a short time it completely stops. Same with anxiety, once you begin to switch it off it will take a few minutes for the feelings to slow and stop.

Introduction: Script #4
Garden Of Your Life

This Script is designed to release negative self-talk, especially those well rooted in a faulty past belief system. We essentially burn these self defeating ideas, beliefs, imprints and inner self talk out of the psyche and plant new seeds of optimism.

This session leads deeper into healing unresolved issues often emanating from childhood. Wounds you may not even remember on a conscious level that continues patterns of behavior that feel as though you are stuck. Often we have ingrained foundational belief systems that constantly tell you things like; you are wrong, you are not good enough, you do not deserve love, success or happiness.

These deep inner feelings began when you were little. Children need parents/guardians for love, support, nurturing, shelter, food, drink and above all safe & protected. We become negatively imprinted when these needs are unfulfilled or if a parent/guardian imposed a type of reward system, such as giving you attention or love when they approve of you or what you did, such as bringing home good grades, or doing your chores correctly, etc. A part of us becomes deeply insecure, and as an adult seeks the approval of others. Many of our relationships can be abusive, where you put up with bad behavior, yelling, degrading you. This is what you experienced as a child, and feels normal to you though none the less hurts. You become trapped in bad relationships and do not know why.

Hypnosis Script #4
The Garden Of Your Life

After induction and deepener..., proceed as follows.

...Imagine that you are now standing in a garden, a garden that symbolizes your life - the garden of your life.... And you are standing there, in the garden of your life, looking around at the trees, the flowers, and the grass, in the garden of your life....

...Feel the warmth of the autumn sun shining down on you... the soft gentle breeze and the perfumes of your favorite flowers.... Notice any shrubs or bushes or other plants...perhaps an ivy-covered archway or one covered in bougainvillea or roses or jasmine.... Perhaps you can hear the birds up there in the trees, whistling their tune to each other.... Imagine it... experience it now ...

...notice the gate leading out of your garden to the street beyond.... You can be happy here in the garden of your life.... But first, I want you to look around and notice here and there the dried up leaves that are scattered around on the floor of your garden.... Some of those leaves are yellow and some are red... in some places the leaves cover the ground almost like a thick carpet, other areas are more sparse. ...

Now those dried up, crumpled leaves are symbolic of all the hurts and frustrations from your life.... Those crumpled, dried up leaves symbolize all the negative conditions from your past and from your present... they represent uncomfortable feelings... feelings of inadequacy... not being good enough... feelings of inferiority or embarrassment ... ...those leaves represent all rebuttals... all refusals... all resentments... all negative statements about yourself, whether made yourself, for yourself... or by others and directed at you....

...All those negative statements that have been made to you at any time in your life are all here in the garden of your life.... Now look over there and see a rake, its long, wooden handle, the rake is propped up and I want you to take that rake and gather together all those dried and crumpled old leaves into a heap, ready to set fire to them...

...And you could give names to some of those dried and crumpled old leaves. Some of the names might represent disagreeable people or events in your life... some may represent subconscious wishes for failure... there may be dislikes for some people in your life... procrastination or past negative conditioning... some may represent laziness or apathy... lack of communication or any spite or hatred or hurt that is held by you for anyone or held by anyone for you....All these negative feelings are scattered on the ground, as you rake them into one big pile, ready for the fire.... And whatever those leaves symbolize to you, we are going to "burn them out of your life, forever".…

...So when the pile is ready, I want you to set fire to those leaves... just enjoy the destruction of all those negativities. ...And as you do, enjoy the feeling of freedom, the feeling of being rid of all those negative influences.... And as you watch the flames leap up into the air you feel all those negative influences from the past leaving you...totally and completely being burnt out of your life....

...It's as though all those negative influences from the past are going up in smoke... and if you look up there you'll see that thick black smoke going higher and higher,... the tail end of the smoke becoming thinner... until it disperses and leaves your life forever.... And suddenly you are free....You are free from all past negative influences, all self-defeating beliefs... all those things that held you back in life... you are free now to progress... to advance... to achieve whatever goals you set out for yourself.... You are free, and it's a wonderful feeling to be free.

...You feel much more confident, much more self-assured, and much more comfortable with yourself....

All past negative influences have departed from your exis-tence and it's as though you can really begin to live again ... to make a fresh start... a healthy... positive start... and continuing to live a fulfilling life doing, not only the things that you have to do every day... but also the confidence and courage to do what you really want to you....

And I want you to experience now... a beautiful violet stream of light pouring down from the blue sky like a laser beam, in through the crown of your head...

Feel and experience a beautiful beam of violet light in through the crown of your head...

...And the violet light symbolizes purity of thought... because now you experience only positive, empowering thoughts and feelings... as far as is humanly possible....

...Feel the light entering the brain... and now streaming down into the spinal column... and out through every nerve... every cell... every fiber... and every consciousness of your being....

...And the purity of thought and feeling touches every nerve and cell and consciousness of your being...filling you with a new healthy energy... a strong and positive empowering energy... and you feel yourself filled with a loving acceptance of the wonderful human being that you are... ...And as you accept the wonderful person that you are, you find that you begin to feel differently about yourself....

...You feel so much calmer...deep deep inside... so much more relaxed... so much more confident... and every cell in your body is bathed in love and acceptance... in a beautiful violet light...

...and your feelings are changing on a cellular level...even between the cells... even altering the chemistry of your body in a positive way...

...Now Autumn and Winter have passed... and it is now a warm Spring sunshiny day.... Out of the garden of your life...you have swept away all those negative thoughts and beliefs that you once held about yourself.... Now according to the laws of nature we have to replenish what we take away... and I want you to see yourself now with a handful of special seeds....

...There is an area of your garden where you instinctively know that these seeds are needed to grow.... The soil is already rich... Fertile... and ready to take those seeds.... So very carefully I want you to tenderly plant those seeds in your garden, with loving care now....

...now sprinkle over the seeds with the soft fine earth....

...now shower the earth lightly to make it moist and then leave the rest to nature.... And as time goes by your seeds will grow and grow and grow....

...Even while they are growing under the earth, you won't

see the shoots until they begin to peep out of the soil ...but you will know that those little seeds have germinated and are sprouting up... you will know because your feelings will tell you so.... You always listen carefully now to your feelings... to your inner self... that wonderful calm and wise and confident self.... Feeling that inner acceptance... loving yourself and who you are in a calm and peaceful sort of way....

In a few moments count up from one to five. At five, you'll be ready to open your eyes and will feel wide awake... but even as you're rousing yourself to become aware to the external world... you know deep inside you that those seeds are already beginning to grow...

Coming Up:

1...Beginning to come up to full alertness... you are mentally alert...emotionally stable and physically stronger and stronger...

from 1 to 2...your mind is clear and calm...your heart is light full soft...your soul is free and at ease ...your body continues to heal and you are happy, content...

from 2 to 3...you will have the best nights sleep tonight... and your sleep will continue to improve...awakening in the morning refreshed...restored...and full of creative energy motivation with fresh ideas...you are always moving in the direction of your optimal health and are the master of your mind and ruler of your body...yes. happiness...all systems in your body function perfectly...

from 3 to 4...take a deep breath as you become aware of your body press upon the bed (chair)...your breathing, body temperature and heart rate are returning to normal...

from 4 to 5 take another deep breath...you are now back to a alert plane of awareness...fully alert and in full control of your mind, full control of your body...remembering, you are the master of your mind, you are the ruler of your body, yes.

Imagine there is a bank account that credits your account each morning with $86,400. It carries over no balance from day to day. Every evening the bank deletes whatever part of the balance you failed to use during the day. What would you do? Draw out every cent, of course? Each of us has such a bank. Its name is time. Every morning, it credits you with 86,400 seconds. Every night it writes off as lost, whatever of this you have failed to invest to a good purpose. It carries over no balance. It allows no over draft. Each day it opens a new account for you. Each night it burns the remains of the day. If you fail to use the day's deposits, the loss is yours. There is no drawing against "tomorrow." You must live in the present on today's deposits. Invest it so as to get from it the utmost in health, happiness and success. The clock is running. Make the most of today.

Thoracic Thump

There is a gland and pressure point at the center of your breast bone. What you do is in rhythm, such as your heartbeat, gently tap, or thump this area for a minute or so. You will notice your breathing calms and deepens, and a sense of serenity spreads throughout your body and stills the mind of unwanted or intrusive thoughts.

Posture

You are a body, mind and spirit/energy, when your posture is curved, such as slumping while standing or sitting, energy becomes entrapped, and often settles in the weakest point in the body. What does that mean? The weakest point in your body is that part most prone to dis-ease. It could be back or neck pain or discomfort, digestive issues, elimination problems, headaches, teeth issues, on and on. Be mindful of your body posture, it is habitual as well as revealing of how you are feeling. Make sure your head is aligned over the rib cage, shoulders slightly back, hips and shoulders aligned. When sitting, make sure you are on your 'sitting bone'. It is in between your tail bone and directly over your anus. You will discover that your breathing is different. At first you may not recognize what a full deep breath is... As any habit, it needs to be unlearned and a new one practiced. I like what is called the string of pearls imagery: Imagine that your spine, neck and head are a string of pearls, and imagine at the crown of your head is the end of the string. Imagine pulling the pearls straight, in alignment. Feel your spine, neck and head perfectly upright, no curves. Become aware of any sway or curve in your back... place your hand at the small of your back and the other hand below your belly button. Tilt your pelvis/hips slowly back until the sway is gone. Now you are in perfect alignment. Women primarily hold this particular body posture. You will find you feel more positive, energetic and have less sick days.

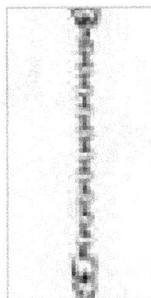

Exercise

Exercise is not a four letter word. Just like anxiety issues, there are varying levels of exercise. It can merely be taking a 15 minute walk. Cleaning, really anything that involves movement of the body for in the least 5 minutes, consider it exercise, and it is essential to your well being in mind, in body, in all ways. You cannot separate your mind from your body, your body from your mind. Your body has certain physical requirements beyond the need for shelter, food, drink. The body needs to move in order to maintain it's overall health. The health in your body reflects the health of your mind. We are creatures of habit. To change a habit you must be willing to either see change as an adventure, or as a place in the land of the uncomfortable. What is the land of the uncomfortable? There is this realm within you from where you live most of your life called the Comfort Zone. From this realm is where you feel most safe, most comfortable, in most control. When we step outside of our comfort zone, we often have thoughts of: 'I am not sure about this." "I am afraid." "What if I fail." etc.

Elements & Minerals

There are crystals that have calming and inner strengthening qualities such as aquamarine, helps with self acceptance and personal strength, feeling comfortable and in command in public and feeling at ease, being in authority. Carnelian, increases sense of self worth and eliminates fear of being inadequate and balances energy. Snowflake obsidian, absorbs negativity as well as hematite. Amethyst, enables one to be present and connected with self and others and highest ideals. Citrine is useful for high energy or frequency people who can't seem to calm down and mental clarity. Lepidolite, which is a secondary component of lithium, I suggest you get it unpolished, when you hold the rock, it's crystals will deposit on your palm and allows it to dissolve into your skin. Moss agate balances overly energized or jitteriness and promotes moderation in one's approach to life rather then a tendency to be either overly expansive or structured. Pick up a gemstone dictionary or go on Google and do some research.

Essential oils, medical grade, can as well be very helpful in managing symptoms, such as lavender to sooth nerves and calm the mind, vetiver, ledum, and then there are companies, such as Young Living Oils, considered one of the best for medical grade essential oils with combinations such as; Peace & Calming, Lavender, Gentle Baby, Inner Child, Grounding, Joy, Hope, Humility.

Citrine   Lepidolite   Snowflake Obsidian

Hemitite   Amethyst   Carnilian

"Tapping," or Emotional Freedom Technique (EFT)

I have known clients, colleagues and friends who have utilized it to release anxiety issues as well, especially those rooted in deep seated anger. I have done general studies and workshops on the subject, and it is based on key acupressure points to release emotional blocks. I can see similarities from key points mentioned earlier in the book with the 'thoracic thump' technique and the benefits.

One of my colleagues here in Arizona, Michelle Lee, CH is an expert practitioner of EFT. I have referred clients with deep seated anger issues who found little or no relief or correction/healing through other modalities. Through her series of 'tapping' sessions, enabled the clients to releasing and finally finding peace.

Emotional Freedom Technique is based on the premise that emotions become stored in the body. When these negative emotions become stored they create a disruption in the body's energy system. By tapping, with gentle pressure on major meridian points all the while focused on the undesired emotion, the disruption is released, thereby releasing the emotion.

Here is how it works:

The Set-up Statement... With this statement you acknowledge the undesired emotion, yet chooses to love, accept and approve of the Self.

For Example:

Even though I am feeling _____ (angry, sad, frustrated, etc)

I deeply and completely love, accept and forgive myself.

This statement is repeated at least three times while tapping the karate chop points together. Michelle says that many people don't even know how they feel. She has also noticed that many women preface the declaration of emotion with, "I know I shouldn't feel this way, but..."

Using the set-up statement gives you permission to feel how you feel and actually be worthy of love, acceptance and forgiveness anyway. After the set-up statement you will move through the sequence.

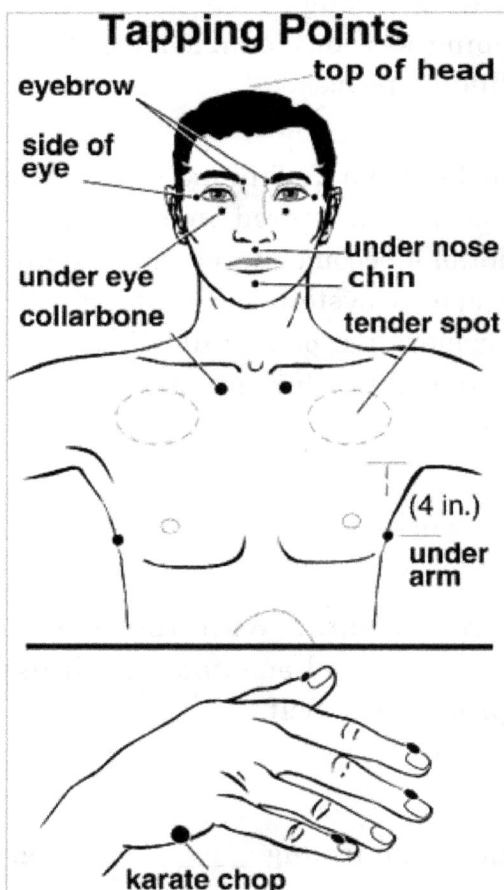

Tapping Points

eyebrow
top of head
side of eye
under nose
chin
under eye
collarbone
tender spot
(4 in.)
under arm
karate chop

The Sequence:

As you tap on the meridian points repeat statements such as; "I feel angry", "I'm sooo angry", I'm pissed off", I hate the way she treats me'" etc. Each time you make a statement you will move to the next tapping point.

1. Karate Chop
2. Inner eyebrow
3. Under eyes
4. Under nose
5. Chin
6. Collar bone
7. Under arm
8. Top of head

1. Karate Chop

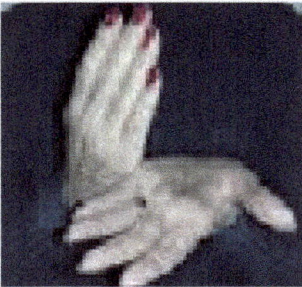

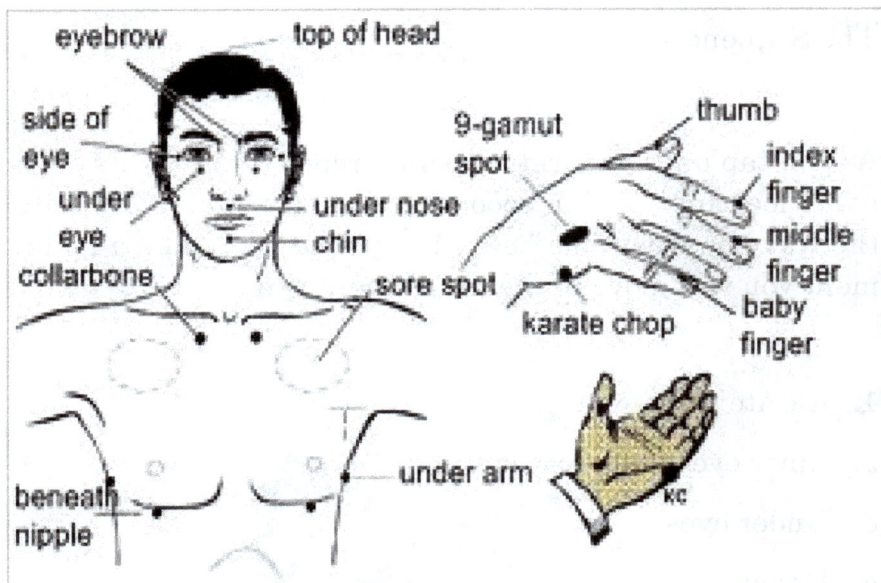

The labels in the diagram:
eyebrow — top of head — side of eye — 9-gamut spot — thumb — index finger — under eye — under nose — middle finger — collarbone — chin — baby finger — sore spot — karate chop — beneath nipple — under arm

The 9-Gamut Procedure:

The 9-gamut procedure is a sequence that can be used when it seems you are stuck in an emotion and can't seem to fully release it. This procedure has proven time and again to be powerful and effective.

After doing a couple of rounds of the basic protocol, you will then tap on the;

1. Karate chop
2. Thumb
3. Index finger
4. Middle finger
5. Ring finger
6. Pinky
7. 9-gamut point

While you tap on the 9-gamut points, you will do the following 9 brain stimulating actions:

1. Eyes closed
2. Eyes open
3. Eyes hard down to the right
4. Eyes hard down to the left
5. Roll eyes in a circle clockwise
6. Roll eyes counter clockwise
7. Hum 2 seconds of a song
8. Rapidly count to 5
9. Hum 2 seconds of a song.

This assists in dislodging a stuck or resistant emotion.

In speaking with Michelle Lee, I asked her how many times does one tap? Her reply was to focus on the emotion as you tap the points and do it as long as it takes or as long as it takes to make the statement, which is about 6 taps.

Perhaps this description and how to of EFT ought to be in the chapter, "Quirky Techniques'" however, these techniques specifically relate to releasing anger, deep angers, not anxiety or panic. It works brilliantly.

Michelle has an excellent program dedicated to freeing teen girls and their mothers from ancient cultural programming to become the leaders they were born to be; Athena Rising Now.

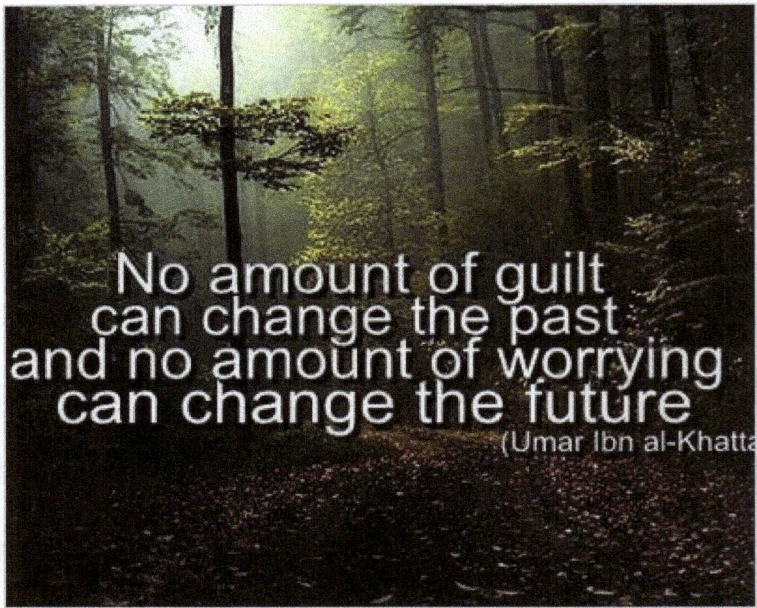

No amount of guilt
can change the past
and no amount of worrying
can change the future

(Umar Ibn al-Khatta

What screws us up most in life is the picture in our head of how it is supposed to be.

We are masters of complicating life, especially when expectations do not meet with our desired reality. Expectations are encapsulated in our belief systems, as well as a projection onto others. Often we become disappointed or worse when our expectations are unmet. We lose faith in others, feeling betrayed or lied to. In our minds when we have an expectation it is a done deal.

Reliance on others, even to keep their word is a slippery slope. The deeper your anger when promises go unfulfilled give you a keener insight as to how much you actually trust yourself. How intense is your anger or disappointment when you yourself do not follow through?

Not long ago I discovered Lao Tzu and I have a common knowledge:

"If you are depressed,

you are living in the past.

If you are anxious,

you are living in the future.

If you are at peace,

you are living in the present."

People often think they are escaping the present, when actually they are retreating into the mind games of time travel. And you are time traveling when focused in the past or future. Your subconscious does not know the difference between imagination or memory based thought processes.

When you focus upon anything not in your immediate now, you are disassociating and in effect removing yourself from the seat of your power, which only resides in the present. If I ask you to show me ten minutes ago, you cannot, unless it is a snapshot or video, but that is still from ten minutes ago, not in the here and now. If I ask you to show me ten minutes from now, you cannot, that is something that is being created from the collective focus you had in the past, and what you are focused upon in the present. So what you have left is the ever spacious present, where you have power, choice to make where you are a pleasure or misery.

Each thought, like raindrops collects, and eventually becomes the nutrients for your seeds to germinate, and thus your garden to grow. Consider your thoughts as raindrops. Your focus as the seeds planted. Where you choose to focus your attentions either creates a deluge, drowning, becoming overwhelmed, or the lack of dreams, desires and goals, finding yourself in a barren, boring place. Make a decision of each thought you allow yourself to focus. In essence, you are nurturing a desire. Even though you may not be thinking of it in that way, it is a truth, it is your truth. You are the master of your mind. Wield your power wisely.

Tip:

If what you are thinking about is not physically in the room with you it does not exist, it is only a thought. Ask yourself; is what I am thinking about something I can control at this moment? If not, let it go or make a note on your "to-do" list.

Eye of the Storm

The Eye of the Storm exercise is a way of focusing and relaxing yourself when life becomes overwhelming. We do not always have control of the circumstances or situations that occur throughout a day but you Can control how you feel & cope & respond. It takes seconds up to 3 minutes and the benefits of being centered, calm, in control and sense of well being will remain long after you finish.

Read the exercise, then stand up and practice it.

While standing imagine with all and every sense you can (visualize, smell, taste, feel, hear) being in a storm, such as a hurricane or tornado.
Within the swirling storm is debris, perhaps elements of your life, issues with loved one, kids demanding your time, challenges in your work place... simply imagine these things/situations in the storm and you are moving, dodging, ducking from being hit by all these things coming at you.

Use your senses; remember the acrid smell of rain?
You can feel the wind whipping, pushing.
You can hear the roar of the wind, perhaps pounding of rain.
You can see items tossed around flying through the air.

Now, take two steps forward into the 'eye of the storm where it is calm and still.
The sky directly above is blue & clear.
Observe the storm now swirling in all directions around you.

Become aware that you are safe here, in the eye of the storm.

Take a few deep breathes while relaxing your jaw, drop your shoulders and relax your belly.

Be mindful of keeping your shoulders relaxed.

Now, bring your attention back to the storm all around you.

Imagine the storm moving away from you in all directions. Notice how the blue sky above expands and you experience the warmth of the sun. Allow the storm to move further and further away from you and dissolve, dissipate, disappearing until you are now surrounded by a beautiful still, bright clear day.

Continue your day.

The subconscious mind responds to pictures, images & symbols.

By practicing this exercise you are *re-setting* and instructing your success mechanism, your subconscious, to release overwhelming responses to whatever is occurring in your life, and it understands that even though these things still exist in your life, you can control, pick and choose in a deliberate, mindful manner what you will focus on.

I call the subconscious *your success mechanism* because it allows you to perform effortlessly throughout your day. Example: You do not need to 'remember' how to ride a bike when you need to go somewhere, you simply swing your leg and straddle the seat and go. Easily previously learned task, habits...such as making a cup of coffee are accomplished without thought...you do not have to *remember* which hand pours from the decanter into a cup, you simply and effortlessly perform the task at hand.

When you practice an exercise such as described, or others presented here, you are programming and reprogramming how you respond... a lot of the time we *react* instead of *acting*, consciously to a situation, challenge, problem or circumstance. When you are calm & mindful, you are always in control, no matter what.

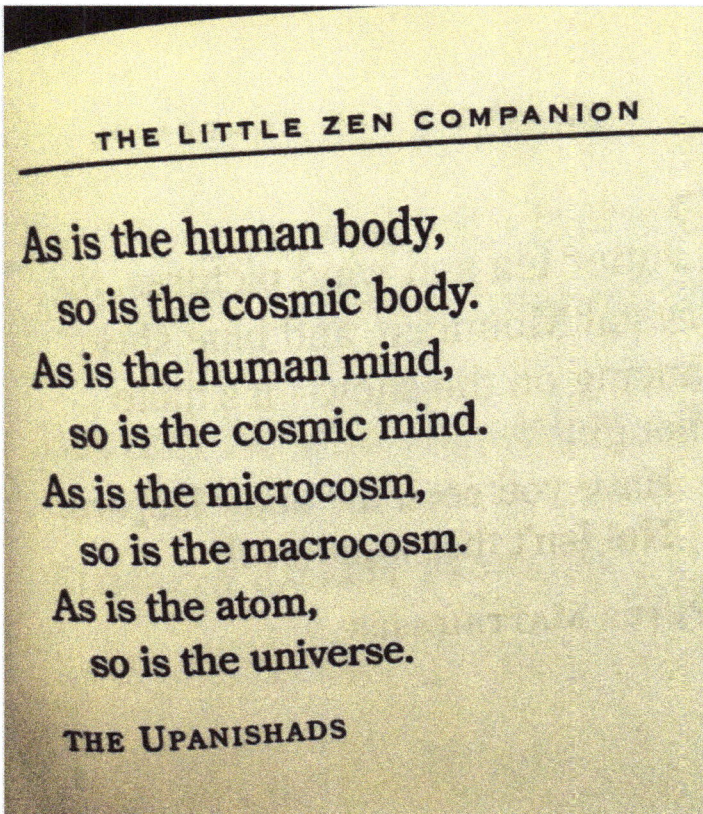

THE LITTLE ZEN COMPANION

As is the human body,
 so is the cosmic body.
As is the human mind,
 so is the cosmic mind.
As is the microcosm,
 so is the macrocosm.
As is the atom,
 so is the universe.

THE UPANISHADS

Sometimes barriers
are just big steps

Kate Ellis,echt

Regret = Guilt and Depression

Like the cat that steals a baby's breath in the middle of the night, in old folk lore, it arrives silently, as a thief invading your home and personal belongings. Digging through draws, overturning carefully placed conveniences donning a home. How violating an experience, to be robbed.

After assessing the devastation comes the coulda, woulda, shoulda's racing through the mind. Did I leave the door unsecured? Should I have had an alarm? Was it time for bad luck to visit? Why me? Insurance won't cover replacement of everything.

It is a totally vulnerable feeling, being robbed. The sense of exposure is raw, cold and unrelenting. Peace of mind, gone. Sadness and anger set in, and paranoia. It can last for a long time. Trust is tested.

Eventually one must begin to rebuild and regroup. Perhaps taking time to choose replacement items with better models. There may be things irreplaceable.

Regret is the thief. It heralds anger, with the self, which often turns inward toward the self, which is the definition of depression.

Regret is plagued with questions that cannot be answered more often than not. Regret is a misuse of guilt, an emotion we all share as human beings.

What is Guilt: It is the foundational beliefs we carry through life. We are taught what is considered right and wrong. Living 'right' brings validation, being accepted and embraced. Living 'wrong' you are bad, shunned, disenfranchised.

Depending on the layers of teachings, your soul could even be at stake.

Guilt is designed to remind us of our foundational beliefs and offers a choice: Either correct your course or expand your beliefs and evolve.

For example; we are taught as children not to cross the street alone, terrible things could happen, fear is instilled to protect you. If however, as you grow and mature you are not taught it is okay to cross at a crosswalk, look left, right then left again, you will continue to go in circles your entire life.

Often we do in many ways, go in circles, as soon as the sensation of fear arises, that is enough to halt most people from examining guilt. Holding on to guilt does not make you a good person. Some believe this type of self flagellation absolves, it does not, it keeps you stuck.

If you carry regrets bordered by guilt, be brave and use the opportunity it provides to reexamine your truth. Ask if you need to grow, to expand. What is this teaching you, you must ask. Is this your truth or one provided for you?

What is important to keep at the forefront of mind as you peruse and examine is (1) That the only place your power or ability to change anything is in the present. You do not have ten minutes ago, it is now a memory. You do not have ten minutes from now, it is still being formed by your actions of the past and present. All decisions and choices exist right here, right now. It is impossible for it to be applied from the past or future.

(2) Another important consideration; more often than not, we are all doing the best we can with what we know in the moment. To apply new knowledge to a past situation is useless.

(3) Your power and choices are in the now.

An expansion of point # 2:

During the deepening process of hypnotizing of a client, I suggested that her muscles were becoming relaxed, numb and comfortable. When I mentioned the word 'numb', I observed a adverse or negative reaction, so I changed the word from numb to soothing. Everything went well and after I brought her up and back, I asked her; "Do you have any idea why you would have a negative reaction to the word numb?" She sat there for a moment, and then nodded her head "yes." After a long pause, I asked her if she wouldn't mind explaining to me. She then said: "I had a child that died. When I found out my child was dead, I went completely numb."

She went on to become a substance abuse counselor. When she learned that substance abuse can escalate from marijuana to other stronger drugs, what is considered 'gateway drugs' she felt a considerable amount of guilt. When raising her child in the 1960's and 1970's, she didn't think her child's experimentation was a big deal. Then when she learned through her training about 'gateway drugs', she felt a considerable amount of guilt. That she was a bad parent. However, you cannot apply new knowledge to past issues with much success. She felt a sense of responsibility in the now, as the child spiraled through drug problems, recovered but eventually committed suicide 20 years in the past. This information was mis-applied. You cannot apply current knowledge to past issues. She did the best she knew at the time, with what she had known. As the saying goes: Hindsight is 20/20.

Another example of guilt:

You are a catholic or Christian, and you are taught that to eat meat on Friday's is a sin.

Every time you forget and have a juicy hamburger on Friday, you feel guilty, and the possibility that you may be jeopardizing your immortal soul. Then you begin to learn more about your religion. And you come across some information about a possible conspiracy of the pope and fishermen in the 15th century. You discover that the fishermen were having a hard time, and that farmers were producing more beef, making it more affordable for the everyday man to put on the supper table. As the story goes the fishermen asked the Pope for help having trouble supporting their families. The Pope declared meatless Fridays, or a new fasting day. Then, as you continue to investigate, you discover that there was no conspiracy between the pope and fishermen but actually it had to do with King Henry the VIII. He fell in love with a woman named Anne Bolen. But, he was married to Catherine. Catherine had not in twenty years bore him a son, and being a ladies man, and needing an aire to the throne, Henry decided he wanted to marry Anne, and asked the pope for a annulment. The Pope, Roman catholic church would not allow it. During those day, the church trumped kingdom, it was a very powerful force in the world. The King could not disobey the church, he made vows. For years a battle ensued. Henry would tell his people that eating fish on Friday was a farce. Eat whatever you want. During those time, Christians regularly fasted, and fish was not considered a meat. Henry never did get the annulment or blessings from the church, no matter what tactic he tried, and eventually broke with the catholic church, overtook the Church of England, divorced Catherine and married Anne.

Now you learn, eating fish or meatless Friday's was not the word of god, but a political issue, an issuance from the Pope. Now, you have the choice to observe your religion or expand your understanding, your soul saved.

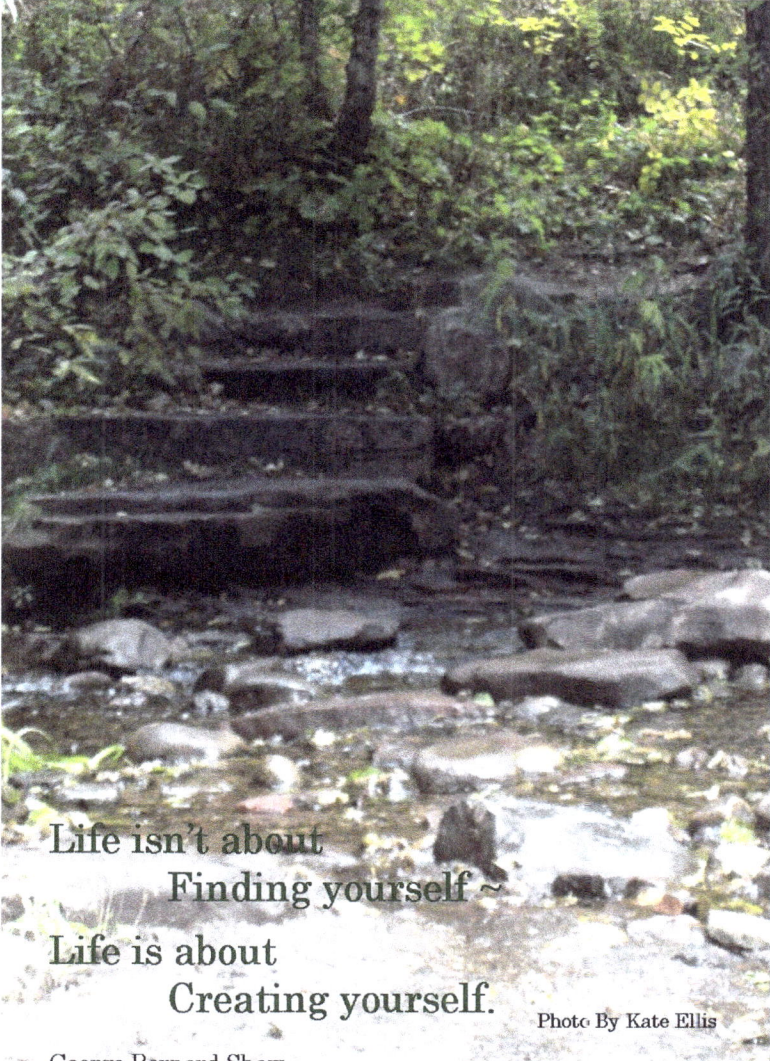

Life isn't about
   Finding yourself ~
Life is about
   Creating yourself.

Photo By Kate Ellis

George Bernard Shaw

KARMA

FEAR-BASED	LOVE-BASED
You reap what you sow. Karma is the consequences, both good and bad, that are brought to you based on your actions, good and bad. You are judged for your actions.	Karma is a gift that brings you lessons for your soul's personal growth, and will continue to bring these lessons back around until you have learned them.

I have an acronym for depression: B.A.D.

Which stands for feeling Betrayed, Angry and Disappointed in or with your self.

This is in essence what depression is; an opinion, decision and/or judgment of yourself.

Remember this:

We are all doing the best we can with what we know, in any given moment. Five minutes from now you may be smarter or wiser.

This throws out the window the woulda, coulda, shoulda's...if you knew better you would have done differently in the past.

You cannot apply current knowledge to the past, because now, you have hindsight and are comparing. Never compare, Aspire.

My personal experiences with anxiety, panic and depression

When I was younger, I was the most unluckiest being upon the planet! I was convinced I did not matter, everything demonstrated this...

I would walk down the street and people would constantly bump into me, as though I was invisible, and not even apologize. I would ask a question, and I was not heard, like I was some sort of phantom.

I would get a job and loose it within weeks or months, no explanation or I was told when being released, my position was temporary while the persons position I filled returned after vacation or leave. Every moment of my life was like I was pushing a mighty river being inundated. This continued for years.

I would pick myself up, try again only to experience over and over again the same luck, the same treatment.

I felt like a waste of space, a piece of dog shit on the bottom of someone's shoes, lower than a worms belly.

I couldn't even be a contributing member of my household financial needs, I felt like a complete burden, and that there were far more other people in the world that deserved to breathe the air, use resources such as food, water.

I had had enough.

I had considered suicide for a long time, seemed to be the answer, make room for someone better than me.

To complicate matters, my brother had committed suicide the year previous. It destroyed my mother. She was a shell of a human being. Then her mother died 1 month after my brother, from a broken heart. Then two cousins got into a fight and stabbed each other to death. Then mom's beloved uncle passed away.

It was a terrible year, 1980. I would constantly check on my mother when she slept, to see if she was still breathing and feared she might loose the will to live.

I was very, very angry with my brother because he beat me to it, and now I am stuck in this wretched fucking place!

Time went by, and drew further away from my brothers death, which I also felt a responsibility for...

...A week or few days, do not recall now, before he did the deed, we were on a long phone conversation. My mother happened to be visiting at the time. He lived in New Jer-sey, we were in Illinois. He begged me to convince mom to move back to NJ. I would have nothing to do with it. All my life I was the weirdo of the small town I was raised in. I was constantly taunted, harassed, bullied, assaulted, teased. There was no way I was going to return to that. I am in a big city now, no one knows me and I am accepted (when I made friends which was rare, I was horribly shy). He was desperate to have his family back together, but I did not understand that. His despair led to that moment of weakness, which I was a party.

Night after night I would perform a ritual of gathering different knives of varying sizes, some serrated, others smooth and wide. I would lay them out in front of me searching for the courage and a mountain of reasons why this was for the best, for me, my mother, who still supported me, everyone.

Night after night I gathered the knives, sat at my desk smoking cigarettes, joints, drinking seeking what I thought was the strength to do this thing, trying to convince myself that to end it would be better for my mother, no longer having to take care of me.

This one particular night, after everyone was asleep, gathered the knives, laid them out in front of me and waited for the impetus. It all finally came together, my mind-set, excuses and especially why my mother would be okay... If you ever experienced the death of a child and its aftermath on a family on the parents, you could understand my great reluctance in inflicting that sort of pain that knows no depths.

I decided. Tonight is the night. I smoked my last joint. I tapped out a cigarette for my last smoke, and as I did, it fell out and rolled on the floor, shit.

I leaned over to pick it up and all of a sudden a brilliant light emerged from the wall in front of me, inside the light was a Being and the Being communicated to me in ways I cannot explain. It told me that I was necessary. It told me it was my attitude that effectuated the experiences I had in life up to that point, that I created my reality, and in order to change it, I needed to change, change my attitude and how I viewed life, people.

The light Being communicated all of this in mid-bow to

grab the cigarette. When I sat back up, the light Being remained for a few more moments, and then disappeared as quickly as it appeared.

I sat there at my desk in a kind of shock.

I sat there for a long time, in a kind of suspension, unable to think.

I became aware of tears running down my cheeks. I put down the cigarette, still unlit and grabbed up the knives, brought them to the kitchen and put them back in their place, like every other night before except, except this would be the last time they would be used this way.

I laid in bed unable to sleep and contemplated everything related to me, and the possibility of the truth of the nature of personal reality revealed to me.

It seemed I was a victim, just trying to defend myself, make a living, walk down the street without being harassed or knocked into without apology.

It was a very long night.

Finally fell into a deep sleep, awoke late the next day still in a shock, in awe, a wonderment.

Was life and most of the experiences I encountered within my control?

How much better if indeed this was true.

A type of hate was suspended for a while inside me, a hate for life and myself. Like I was placed in neutral from my belief system which was largely based of course of my experiences.

I wanted to believe that this is true. I did not want to cause my mother pain. I was not sure I did want to live, but if I could do one right thing in my life and honor my mother, I would prefer to live than to cause her pain.

I began to come across books that spoke about attitude, and how it created attributes of personal reality, I studied, read and practiced.

Did everything change over night? NO! No it did not, it actually was the road to a new journey of discovery.

I took a chance that the light Being, who emanated this light that somehow embraced me, did not judge me.

And I began again.

The process of changing took years, not too many though. I began to see results, or the consequences of my actions, and the Beings instructions and information appeared to be true, I did create my reality in what I thought about, focused upon, my perception and attitudes.

Life became better, a bit more easier and yes, still struggles, but a tolerable one for the most part.

I still had a way to go as the years passed, but I continued to learn, delved deeply into science, quantum physics, spirituality.

As I opened my mind and heart, I found what I needed almost magically. But it is not magic. There is a scientific and universal law: Like attracts like. Very simple, but oh so potently true.

As I shifted my perception, focus, thoughts and attitude, experiences in life reflected that back to me.

So I say to you, as I have a very intimate understanding of this, if you are breathing, you are Necessary. Even if you have no idea why, if your life sucks, you have no friends, you do not recognize the people who love you.

You create your reality by the thoughts you choose to focus upon. YES, you choose your thoughts. You either choose to focus upon them or let them slide on by, it is always your choice.

That is another important thing about life; choice and change. Everything is in constant flux, no day is ever exactly the same, and it changes in direct relation to what you choose to think. Your thinking creates the feeling you then have, and focused thought and feeling creates the motion of emotions.

To extricate yourself from gloom, sadness, fear, pain... change the focus of your thoughts and everything will shift. Learn everything you can about the nature of reality. My studies furthered when I read the book by Jane Roberts: "The Nature of Personal Reality."

It may not be your cup of tea, Dr Wayne Dyer may have the key to unlock the bolts of that door within your mind you have fastened to protect you that also locks out the possibility of happiness, control, loving relationships.

It may be Carolyn Myss, or Louise Hay or Joseph Campbell or Richard Bach. If you Google "attitude" I wonder what might pop up on your screen, I have not tried it yet... But it is a start, a resource for you to understand and begin to take control back of your life, your heart and your place in this world, because you are here and I know you are necessary.

Tell yourself:

Everything
will work out.

Things will get better.

You are important.

You are worthy
of great things.

You are loveable.

The time is now.

This too, shall pass.

You can be who you
really are.

The best
is yet to come.

You are strong.

You can do this.

We believe
what we tell
ourselves.

Master your mind, don't be mastered by it.

Your mind is a tool.

Experiments

Correcting a panic dis-order is really the easy part. Now you must turn your attentions not only to the thoughts that created the continuation of fear messages which then tripped the fight/flight/freeze response, but begin to untangle your anxieties. This takes a little time, a lot of attention and practice, practice, practice.

I am listing experiments for you to practice and embrace for all they are worth. You need to shift your sense of self perception. We have touched on this throughout the book, and now it is time to be proactive and take specific actions to change from a worrier to a Warrior.

You will accomplish this by working on these experiments, and whole heartedly apply them to your life and choice of experience in your life, within your mind and creating an attitude which will serve your highest good, aspirations, dreams and desires. What is important to take note of is that as you practice suspending an old belief, pattern of behavior, reactions to the situations and circumstances in and around your life, whether you are in control of the situation, or merely have the choice of response, above all practice patience with yourself. It may have been years upon years you have cultivated your/the anxieties. Consider it may take as long to shift. It really does not. Often I suggest treating new shifts in perception and attitude like a pregnancy; treat this unborn life as gently and mindfully as possible. Paying attention to what you eat, drink, ingest, permit...

Ask yourself will this help this new life to develop healthily or could it be harmful affecting this new life for all of it's days?

An experiment in Self-Trust:

What if you decided for a week, seven days, to trust yourself, your decisions, your intuitions, your own voice over any others?

This means to suspend second guessing yourself, to make a decision and not look back. Accepting that there is a possibility you may be wrong, may make an error, may make a mistake. With this acceptance of these considered possibilities, you recognize that in order to reach an ideal, mistakes, errors are par for the course. It is said Rome was not built in a day, and you can imagine that construction did not always go smoothly, but never the less, it did get done.

Going further with this experiment, to build self-trust, employ a list method. Make a To Do list as exampled earlier in this book, list the priorities of the day... of the day. Then use the list to guide your day, marking off your accomplishments. It does not matter how mundane or routine they may be, or even attending to things you may have procrastinated on in the past. With giving yourself permission to trust yourself, and that you may make errors, you do not burden yourself with ideas or expectation or demands of perfection. You may find that you have the courage to begin what you consider a difficult task, and it does not totally work out. It is okay to begin a task, get stuck, walk away and begin again.

Example: I recently videoed via my very first smart phone

a presentation. I am now tasked with editing the video, I have very little experience editing. I thought about it for a day or so, knowing this is going to be tedious. Eventually I began to tackle this challenge, and spent a few productive minutes figuring out this new device and what it could do. I also spent many more minutes making many mistakes, and by the time I put the smart phone down was not too close to my objective. But I began, learned a little and will once again attempt to accomplish my goal. I am also considering asking someone with more experience for assistance. It is an option. However, I will later in the day return to the project, holding in mind it is a great challenge for me, and with this acceptance greatly reduce any frustration that accompanies what I consider daunting.

This moves us into another experiment, Expectation:

Often we feel either; **B**etrayed, **A**ngry or **D**isappointed by or of ourselves when we do meet with our expectations. This comes from an internal expectation, and it may be the voices or echoes of your parents, peers, a person you aspire or would like to mirror or impress, and when you do not perceive you have made the mark, reached the bar, done something right these feelings of "B.A.D." arise, sometimes with a vengeance!

In our minds, expectation means it is a done deal, and when things veer off the anticipated course, frustrations can arise and we feel B.A.D. What is worse, we may equally project upon loved ones, family, friends the same voracity of expectations, and when they fall short again, B.A.D. comes into play.

I suggest to anticipate, not expect. With anticipation it is less demanding within the psyche, self perception and frustration levels when life does not meet with what you envision. This is a poster I have hanging in my office:

What screws us up most in life is the picture in our head of how it is supposed to be.

Especially when others do not meet up with our expectations, perhaps they have given their word, and still do not follow through, then you must consider how consistent they are. If a person continually disappoints you, ask yourself: Has this person been consistent in their behavior or follow through. Ask yourself: Am I beating a dead horse? Ask yourself: Am I expecting this person to carry my responsibilities? To have control, accept 100% responsibility for your life. If you own it, you can change it.

A personal experience of dealing with expectations:

During my marriage I carried the load of maintaining the household chores, which includes grocery shopping, laundry, cleaning, yard maintenance, meal preparation, hand washing dishes transporting our child, work outside the home, school and the care and feeding of my husband. My husband was delegated two duties within the household; taking out the garbage and changing the kitty litter. Even though I felt there was still an inequity in the distribution of responsibilities, he was the main bread winner, and these two chores are not terribly taxing.

Unfortunately, my husband was not terribly attentive or interested in helping out. It became a regular argument, so much so I could have taped it and simply hit the play button. No matter what I did or did not do to heal this rift, nothing worked; more sex, less sex, making an agreement, pleading, calmly asking, not so calmly asking. Nothing changed the situation.

One day, after having yet another argument, I sat down at my desk and angrily remarked to myself; "That man is amazingly consistent!" Then the light bulb went off in my head. Yes, yes... my husband is totally consistent, no matter what I do, nothing changes. I thought about how I justified to myself just doing it myself, I thought I would feel resentful towards him, picking up yet another chore to add to my already heavy load. Then I thought; is this worth losing my marriage? There was a terrible wedge between us over the sense of inequity and other feelings such as; if he loved me he would.... Fill in the blank.

I came to the conclusion that I would rather risk the resentment over the possible ending of my marriage. Right then and there I decided to make a sign to hang over my desk: "Just Do It! Now mind you, this is before the Nike campaign.

I took this message to myself to heart, and every time I thought he should do something or step up, I looked at my sign. Every time I thought about doing something and considered putting it off just as quickly, I would look at my sign and jump into action instead of pondering about it, then feeling B.A.D. about it, no matter how mundane or lofty. I began accomplishing a lot from then onward.

Another curious thing occurred once I made and stuck to this decision and attitude: Not only was I a happier woman with a clean kitchen and no stinky garbage or cat litter, my husband actually began helping out, without me asking. He would spontaneously take out the garbage, or grab it from me after tying it off. What I had feared all along actually did not occur.

So often our fears do not come into fruition, yet they keep us stuck just the same. Sometimes we are so hyperfocused on what we believe might happen, we do not trust ourselves to do the things for ourselves what will create comfort. If you are in a marriage or partnership, and you find the same issues go round and round, consider letting go of your resentments, fears and exasperations, and just do it yourself. Assume one hundred percent responsibility of what does and does not get done. When you assume one hundred responsibility of your life, you can then change it, because you own it outright.

Experiment: Home is where your hat is:

Often people can feel anxious outside of their comfort zone, such as one's home or area of travel, such as work or a local store, places that are familiar. When outside of those boundaries can arise a sense of being unbalanced, out of your element, perhaps jittery or avoiding unfamiliar places altogether. This occurs most often when anxiety turns into agoraphobia. To begin to change this, to be able to reclaim your life and your place in the world you have to know you are safe no matter where you go, whether alone or with others.

There is an old saying: Home is where your hat is. This may come from early in the 20th century when a properly dressed person, man and woman alike wore hats. When one took off their hat and placed it down, it meant they were welcome or in a place of safety or "home", where one can be at total ease. It also means you 'own' or are in control where you are at. So, whether your issue is driving on a highway or new place, going to a social event in public or a friends home, whether you are taking a meal by yourself or a movie, whatever has vexed you in the past, imagine that you are wearing a hat, imagine taking it off and placing it beside you and stating to yourself: Home is where my hat is." You will find it remarkable and amazing how comfortable you begin to feel.

Experiment with Time:

Time has been spoken a lot in this book, it is the crux of anxiety issues. Often we do not realize we are displacing our power of now by focusing in the past or in the future... Remember what Lao Tzu said...

Begin this week long experiment the moment you wake up. If you are keeping a dream journal, first attend to that. Then, as you are laying there, begin to think about the things in your life you are grateful for. Just of those things you have, they may not be perfect, but that is not what this experiment is about. State gratitude for having shelter, transportation, family, friends, a job, your health, etc.

You may not be in the home you like, but that is not what this is about. You have shelter, you are dry when it rains, warm when its cold, running water, a refrigerator... those basic things. You may not be driving the best car at the moment, but it gets you from here to there, or the bus or train, it may not be your vision of ideal, but again, this is not what this experiment is about. It is about acknowledging what you have in a mindful manner.

When you acknowledge your blessings, what you have with gratitude, it creates joy, which releases those good endorphins and oxytocin. Perhaps consider keeping it at the forefront of your mind the entire day, discovering all the things you have right now. Do not dwell on what you do not have. When you focus on the now, you become fully present.

Experiment with resetting your circadian rhythm ~ Sleep:

For many people unrelenting thoughts inhibits getting to sleep or staying asleep or upon awakening immediately feel the pangs of anxiety or lack of restoration. First you will want to have a journal; Thoughts of the Day. This is a place where you simply write down what you did, your thoughts and experiences. It is a place to get the things that may or may not be bothering you out of your head and on to paper, before going to bed

Second, review your to do list, check off what has been accomplished. If there are things you have not done, reprioritize, ask yourself if you really need to do this and if so, decide its place on the morrows list. Create a to do list for the following day, list your three to five priorities, and other things you need or want to get accomplished. It may contain elements of a grocery list, mundane items such as banking, picking up the kids from school, preparing dinner, begin your thesis... Again, getting things out of your head, from your thoughts on to paper in which you can refer to. I suggest this is done away from your bed. Begin to make your bed a place for sleep and sex. Retrain your brain that when you lay down for the evening, or whenever your sleep time is, that once your head hits the pillow, it indicated and instructs, time to sleep.

It is okay if you have a ritual of perhaps reading, or watching tv having set the sleep timer on the tv. If you need to add to your list, sit up at the edge of your bed and add to it, not lying down. You might consider turning your phone off or on silent. If you are not an emergency worker, or have an obligation to be available, create a zone of time that is exclusively yours, a do not disturb time. This is your responsibility, no one else's. So if you do not have pressing obligations, let it go to voice mail. Create a type of sanctuary which is under your control. Sometimes we need to create boundaries by being proactive. I have had clients who decide to tell people, look, between this and this time do not disturb me, and then become angered that it is not honored. This is totally silly, you are the one who chooses to answer the phone or not. You are in control of your world, so claim responsibility.

To reset your circadian rhythm, or sleep cycle: Lay down, tuck yourself in and get in a comfy position. You may want to imagine you are embraced or covered by a white light or cloud or bubble or sheet. Or you may want to use the color of violet. What this does is reinforce that you are safe and protected. You may want to state an affirmation:

"Every day in every way I am better and better...I am stronger, confident, calmer and wiser, I am healthier in mind and body alike... I am forgiving of myself and others, I trust myself and inner guidance... I view every situation and circumstance as an opportunity to grow and accomplish my goals and accept the unexpected assisting me to open my mind and heart which allows me to evolve... my control is my attitude, I am the power in my world."

Employ the reset button technique. After you become a bit more comfortable and somewhat relaxed, you may want to begin a progressive relaxation technique, instructing the parts of your body to become loose and limp, release all tension in every muscle, tendon and tissue from toe to head or head to toes. Then, as you inhale think of the phrase; At Ease. As you exhale think of the word;

Relax or Sleep or Peace. Continue to think "At Ease" as you inhale, and "Sleep" or "Relax" or "Peace" as you exhale until you slip into sleep.

You will find that at times your mind will begin to wander, and you discover that you forgot about the exercise. Your job at this point is to simply return to the exercise. Do not become frustrated. It is called a practice for a reason.

You may also find that amazing ideas arise. State to yourself: I will remember this at the appropriate time, and then return to your practice.

It takes three to ten days to reset your circadian rhythm, and you will not have issues sleeping through the night again.

Upon awakening in the morning, allow your first thoughts to be on gratitude, that you are safe and the day is full of opportunities. You may want to have the song; Oh what a beautiful morning ring through your mind if there is instant chatter upon awakening. Decide the flow and content of thoughts. Remember, what you focus upon you empower.

> You were born
> to win, but to be
> a winner you must
> plan to win,
> prepare to win,
> and expect to win.
>
> Zig Ziglar

Experiment Expanding
Beliefs by; What If's:

What If's are a powerful, potent thought. It is a powerful and potent aspiration. What If is a powerful and potent decision. You could perhaps consider a decision as a process. Movement, one step and then another,

And another.

W.I ~ I respond differently

> I trust myself & not second guess

> Make a choice/decision and not look back

> Own choice

W.I ~ There is no wrong decision?

W.I ~ I rely only on myself & no one else

> Assume total responsibility for every nuance of this day.

W.I. ~ I choose not to react with anger

> No matter what, Today ~

> Be mindful, not reactionary

Example: One morning barely awake, I stumbled down the stairs, I don't necessarily wake up purty, coffee, coffee echoing in mind and drift towards the machine. A nice cup o java the only presence of mind...   Recently, we had this gnat invasion, beasts. The source was discovered and amended. Remnants remained, a few dozen perhaps. Autopilot ensued; kill gnats.

I arrived at the little corner carved out on the counter exclusively for the art of coffee making.   Turned on the Keureg, grabbed the coffee grinds, filter, vessel and cap. Dreamily went about filling the filter with a deep, dark, just bitter enough bean.   Gnats came into my field of awareness, and focused on one dancing above my fingers holding the designed morning fare... A determination of eliminating the beast momentarily captured my attentions, and as soon as it lingered, I would pounce... the opportunity arrived, and (near) involuntarily swatting with my left hand, full of the most delicious beans... It's fine grind splashed across the counter and down to the floor. There was an uncomfortable feeling, with a side of anger. Stood there a moment, taking it all in, then asked myself; are you going to get angry and , and... or blow it off and make a cup of coffee? Lamenting that to throw a tizzy expends an enormous amount of energy, no good.   Just be amused and make coffee.   I amuse myself constantly. So...

I first cleaned up the grounds, there was an outline of my foot in coffee grounds, there were grounds between my toes, if I intended to make that much of a mess, couldn't have done much better. I then made the cup o java and escaped upstairs, leaving the incident behind me watching the morning news.

Your reactions are not out of your control, they are indeed programmed, however by you, you created a reaction, you can un-create it or create an entirely new one.

W.I ~ You are the only power in your world, and you either choose to wield it or give it away?

W.I ~ You own today?

W.I ~ I celebrate this day?

W.I ~ These experiences with anxiety, panic and depression contains unseen gifts?

> The gift of understanding my powers.

> The gift of recognizing nothing can control me unless I give permission.

> I am not a victim, I have not trained my mind.

W.I ~ Today, I take back my power and learn how to use it for my highest good?

W.I ~ I choose to make the decision each and every day to act in a mindful manner?

W.I ~ I decide to be the mind or thought police for a while and become cognoscente of my thoughts and feel ings and when I find my words or language or feel ings are not empowering me I will change it. Like I have a chalk board in my mind, I can erase the 'I'll try' to I will;

> 'I should' to just do it; 'Why me' to I will make this situation or circumstance, my life work.

W.I ~ I am infinitely patient with myself.

W.I ~ I am patient with others.

On the following pages, you could place the What If (W.I.) in front of the sentence, especially if you are challenged believing the assertions at first, until you prove them for yourself.

You are the master of your mind.

You are not an accident.

You chose this life for the experience and to master your energy

Your life and presence is necessary (otherwise you would move on).

Life will always work to move you to your highest good.

Intuition is the expression of Divine Source and is the highest form of truth.

Your ego is a tool, and must be used correctly.

Your subconscious is like an automatic program which allows you to operate smoothly in the world... and you are the ultimate programmer by what you choose to believe.

As children we are given a general program, as an adult, you can re-write programs that no longer suit your desires and aspirations.

Your breath controls your state of body, mind and clear connection to your intuition.

Your imagination creates reality.

Your focus attracts experiences.

If you choose the view that everything is an opportunity, amazing things happen.

To be a victim is to give away your power.

You are a spirit having a human experience.

There are no mistakes, only mis-takes.

No one has power to create in your life or you in others.

All life is precious.

There is no such thing as positive/negative, good or bad and sometimes right or wrong this is based on you perception.

You have two purposes in life, the ones you chose by choosing this life and from Divine Source.

When your purposes are fulfilled you will transition back to spirit/energy.

You cannot bargain or make a deal with Divine Source, only make decisions and follow through.

Prayer works.

Each thought is a prayer.

Time is a luxury or gift, allowing space for your manifestations.

We all have roles.

We need to learn to discern, not judge.

People in our lives are attracted, agreed upon and serve as lessons.

There are master teachers, such as Jesus, Buddha, Rumi, Mother Theresa, etc. that serve as reminders not guru's.

You can shift genetic propensities.

The entire world and all of its inhabitants are sentient and we all feed off one another... animals, plants, water, etc.

Send anonymous Blessings often, in thought, in deed.

When you change yourself you change a part of the world.

The butterfly effect is real.

As spirits having a human experience, rituals are important as we are bathed in foundational belief systems.

Your life and concerns count and you do make a difference.

There are angels among us.

Everything around you was a thought in somebody's mind become manifest.

Miracles are lack of resistance or life unimpeded.

Meditation/silence (inner) is vital such as sleep, food, shelter, water and love is.

Focus on desires directs experience... often we focus on what we do not want... often we get stuck on the how (often we test, create drama).

To risk, to be vulnerable (confident) is trust in action.

In life we serve awards, ultimately, this, life, is not a reward system.

Balance is not static.

Old beliefs are like echoing voices, merely thoughts... choose what thoughts you focus on.

Attitude is your latitude.

To attain knowledge, add things every day... To attain wisdom, remove things every day.

Let go of your past to succeed in your future & present.

Eliminate negative thoughts, feelings and self talk, allow them to serve as red-flags that you are either angry, betrayed or have not lived up to a personal expectation.

Accept, believe & anticipate success.
To worry about tomorrow is to forfeit your peace today.

Eliminate your fear of change. Yes.

Make peace with your inner critique, it is after all an echo of you, allow it to be your ally and best friend a greatest supporter.

Wake up your motivation, just do it.

Will power does not work long term.

Program your mind for success.

When you think about the past or future you are time traveling essentially and displacing your power that lives in the present.

Change your autopilot.

Worry places your body on a constant state of alert, which is damaging and accelerates aging and promotes dis-ease which will occur at the weakest point in the body.

If it isn't in the room with you, it is not threatening you, worry is about your ability to feel safe and in control in the future.

You can rewire your brain and ultimately mind.

Make changes from practice to permanent.

Don't limit your challenges, challenge your limits.

Everything, every situation, every circumstance provides an opportunity... you can choose to accept, avoid or struggle.

You get out of life what you put in it.

Expectations can be harmful from yourself and of others, anticipation is often better.

You accept what you expect.

The only limitations in life are what you accept.

It's only a thought, and a thought can be changed.

Resentment, guilt and criticism are damaging patterns and often emerge in the body as disease.

Release the past and forgive everyone, including yourself.

Accept yourself and all of your beauties and flaws.

Relationships are a compliment to you, not a completion of your soul or self or life.

When you accept yourself as is, embrace the you that is in a constant state of evolution, everything in our life works (for your highest good).

Universe does not judge, life is about balance/karma.

If you have a belief system in good & bad, saintly or evil and you will be ultimately judged, also remember that there is always an opportunity to balance and be forgiven, in every religion this is so.

No matter where you go, there you are.

An old Cherokee told his grandson, "My son, there is a battle between two wolves inside us all.

One is Evil. It is anger, jealousy, greed, resentment, inferiority, lies and ego. The other is Good. It is joy, peace, love, hope, humility, kindness, empathy, & truth."

The boy thought about it, and asked, "Grandfather, which wolf wins?"

The old man quietly replied, "The one you feed."

– author unknown

Be *Yourself*.

Nobody is better Qualified.

Your subconscious is literal. It believes every-thing you think, state and how you hold your body language.

It is similar to a 4-6 year old child. If you tell the child there is a tooth fairy, they will re-spond with; "what does she look like, what will she give me?

If you said to that child the things you think about yourself, would it encourage or break their spirit?

Gratitude unlocks the fullness of life. It turns what we have into enough and more. It turns denial into acceptance, chaos to order, confusion to clarity. It can turn a meal into a feast, a house into a home, a stranger into a friend. Gratitude makes sense of our past, brings peace for today and creates a vision for tomorrow. --Melody Beattie

The trick is in what one emphasizes. We either make ourselves miserable, or we make ourselves happy. The amount of work is the same. --Carlos Castaneda

One does not become enlightened by imagining figures of light, but by making the darkness conscious. --Carl Jung

Knowing others is intelligence; knowing yourself is true wisdom. Mastering others is strength; mastering yourself is true power.

Living with integrity means: Not settling for less that what you know you deserve in relationships. Asking for what you want and need from others. Speaking your truth, even if it might create conflict or tension. Behaving in ways that are in harmony with your personal values. Making choices based on what you believe, not what others believe. --Barbara De Angelis

Don't worry about the people in your past--there's a reason some of them didn't make it into your future.

You cannot know your own perfection until you have honored all those who were created like you. A Course in Miracles

At some stages you will experience a plateau, as if everything had stopped. This is the hard point in the journey. Know that once the process has started it doesn't stop; it only appears to stop from where we are looking. Ram Dass

CONFIDENT vs. ARROGANT
ENTREPRENEUR   ENTREPRENEUR

TALKS TO POWERFUL PEOPLE
because he doesn't doubt
the value of his ideas

TALKS TO POWERFUL PEOPLE
because he wants to be
seen as one

ADMITS IGNORANCE
because he doesn't doubt his intellect

SHOWS HE IS RIGHT
because being wrong hurts his
credibility

APPROACHES STRANGERS
because he doesn't doubt the value
of his company and conversation

WORKS THROUGH HIS NETWORKS
because he already knows
they accept him

**ACTS LIKE A FOOL
WHEN FEELS LIKE IT**
because he doesn't doubt his worth

**ACTS LIKE HE IS CONFIDENT
ALL THE TIME**
because otherwise people might
stop taking him seriously

Funders and Founders

May the sun bring you new energy by day, may the moon softly restore you by night, may the rain wash away your worries, may the breeze blow new strength into your being. --Apache Blessing

Those who love you are not fooled by mistakes you have made or dark images you hold about yourself. They remember your beauty when you feel ugly; your wholeness when you are broken; your innocence when you feel guilty; and your purpose when you are confused. --African saying

There is a force in you that is more powerful than the negative people, circumstances or environment you find yourself. Make a conscious deliberate effort to keep your mind above all the toxic conversations, attitudes and stressful atmosphere surrounding you.

Guard your mind by immersing yourself in positive words, scriptures, music; as well as self-affirming healing conversations that will drown out the negative voices within your own mind.

Create a ritual of prayer, meditation, exercise, yoga, Tai-Chi, volunteering of your time, or whatever methods you can use that will protect you from the drama, emotional vampires and energy drainers that will try to rob you of your peace.

There is a Presence within you where you can find joy, comfort and inner strength to give you the capacity to handle whatever you are facing. You have GREATNESS within you! Les Brown

It is not because things are difficult that we do not dare; It is because we do not dare that they are difficult. Seneca

Every man take the limits of his own vision, for the limits of the world. Arthur Schopenhauer

Whether you think you can or whether you think you can't, either way you are right. Henry Ford.

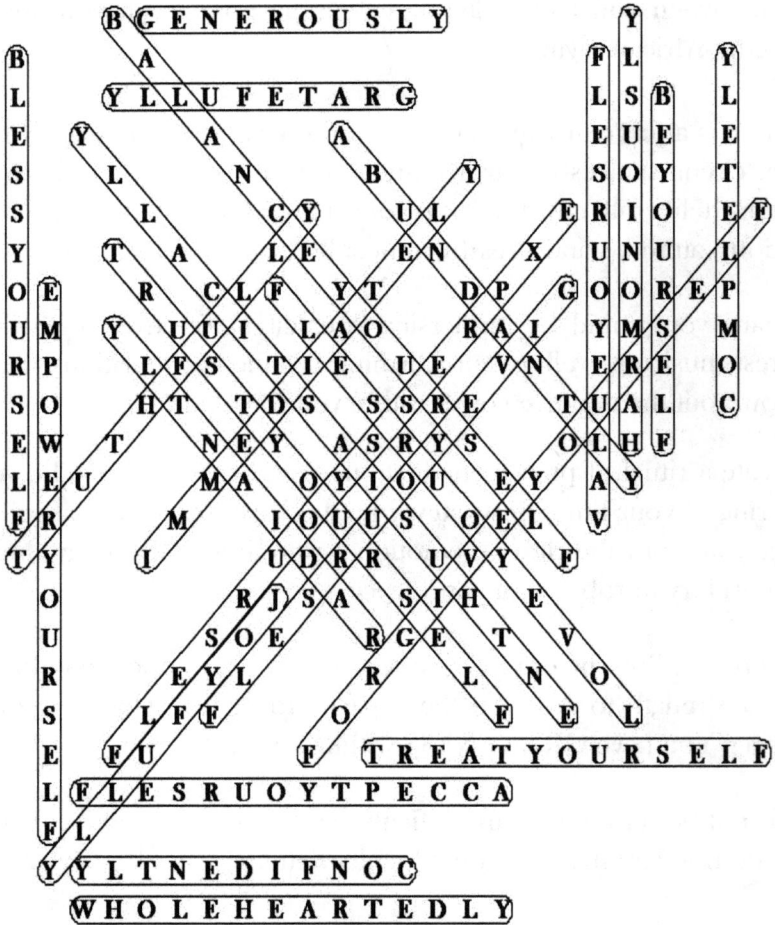

Story as a Vehicle

Our stories of experience are vehicles. The story itself is not always meant to be repeated, regurgitated, re-lived, in many ways it is holding on to the past, or a way to define ourselves, through our stories of life's experiences. Sometimes we cling dearly to our stories, which keep us stuck, especially if there is still an emotional charge attached. Often we know that we have assimilated a difficult experience when upon telling the story a reaction or feeling is no longer present, it is but a story.

Many of us do not recall how we learned what the term "hot" meant. Our parent as we became more mobile may have warned; don't touch the stove, it is hot, or don't touch the radiator, it's hot or don't eat the soup, it is still hot. As children, we do not have the experience yet of what hot is, so we recognize the sense of caution from the parent, but still not able to grasp what they mean. Then at some point you touch the stove or eat the soup and burn your mouth. Now you have an experience of 'hot'. And as time winds on you learn of other categories of hot, such as fire, pots and pan handles, a mug of hot chocolate. We learn to respect hot in all of it's guises. However, most of us do not recall the first experience of learning what hot is. That is because it does not matter, it is the experience and knowledge which is of importance, not how you learned, but what you learned.

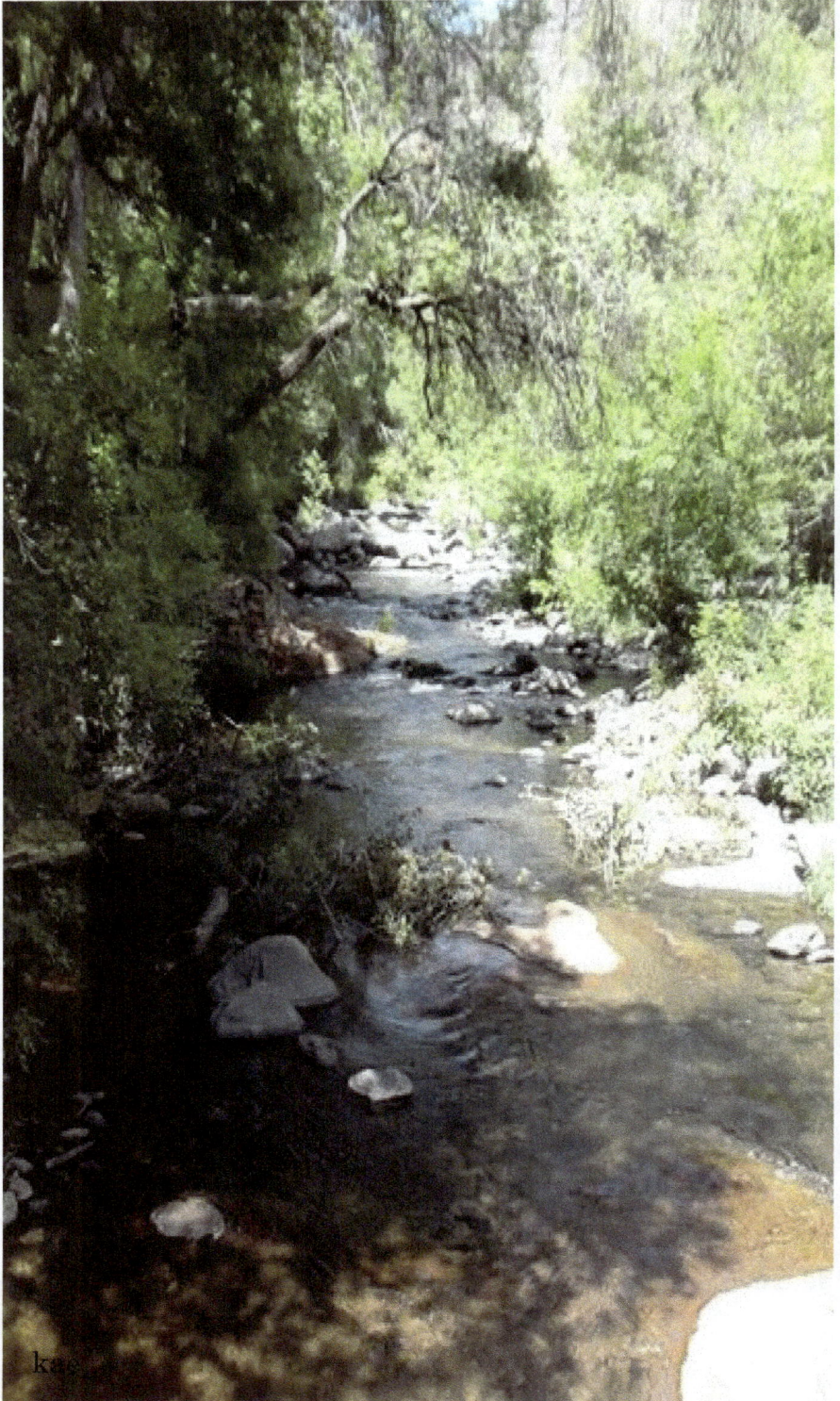

Worrier to Warrior, Conquer Anxiety and Panic Attacks

MP3 Program & Books

Worrier to Warrior:

This MP3 introduces you to anxiety/panic attacks and anxiety dis-orders. Anxiety & Panic attacks, also called 'dis-order' is highly correctable and, there is an enormous gift from the ordeal...

The (WTW) Metanoia MP3 presents comprehensive information, tools and techniques on understanding the nature of anxiety/panic and why I call it a "thinking dis-order" not a permanent form of mental illness. Ask yourself: What if...my mind is mastering me instead of me mastering my mind, which is a tool?

You will have an understanding of what is happening to you, and how to begin to manage not only the symptoms of anxiety/panic, but realize that your world, your life needs not be limited in any way, shape or form. This is the first phase of correcting anxiety/panic attacks.

If you are taking medications for symptom relief, you will discover it is not a life sentence, and anxiety/panic is correctable, not unlike a broken bone, once it is set and the body heals, it is now stronger. **Important note here;** Do Not stop taking medications on your own, talk to the clinician prescribing them for instructions. Many meds these days you cannot simply stop taking, there can be devastating effects if done improperly, trust me. Be responsible and proactive.

You now enter "Metanoia" (n) which means; the journey of changing one's mind, heart, self and way of life.

Mind-Spa Ultimate Healing MP3

The Mind-Spa session is specifically designed to release, and transmutes old, inhibitive energies, beliefs, past impressions in perceptions. We sometimes unknowingly hold on to past emotional issues in our energy fields, within the subconscious as well as in the body. Do you have aches or pains that do not appear to have any known origin?

Are you doing your utmost best to create changes, but find little or limited success? Are your energies low, like you are suffering from an exhaustion, yet do not feel you are expending that much energy to warrant feeling worn down...What about your weight, does it seem to have a mind of its own, fluctuating beyond your best efforts. Do you find yourself procrastinating, putting things off or simply not wanting to deal with issues, situations in your life, even though you know better?

If you have some or all of these issues, you are carrying around emotional debris, emotional baggage.

I like to describe it like this: We all have a receptacle, or garbage can within our home. Once it fills up, we then take the garbage out to a larger trash can to be taken away. Sometimes, after we have sorted through issues in our lives, and we have moved beyond them, we still seem haunted by having challenges in manifesting our decisions. This is because somehow you 'forgot' to take out the trash in the house for it to be taken away.

Once you experience the Mind-Spa Session, you will have immediate relief; feel physically lighter, as though a heavy burden has been lifted off of your body, your being. You will experience fresh energy, creative vitality and new ideas to align you with your highest good.

If you are having financial, career issues, new avenues open up. If you are having issues with communications with loved ones, friends, co-workers or your staff, you will find and discover new in-roads and ability to effectively communicate what you want from others, and allow others to hear your needs.

If you are experiencing issues with sleep, organization and focus these as well begin to shift, and you find you are balanced in body, mind and energy/spirit. These are some of the wonderful benefits you will achieve and experience.

Mind-Spa has two tracks, one with the hypnosis session, the second are 50 plus affirmations to correctly state your intentions that creates and promotes self confidence, self esteem, self awareness and self sufficiency. Only the second affirmation track can be used safely while preparing for the day, or as subliminal background noise or in your car.

If you are taking medications: Once you feel the shift in your life, and the lack of anxiety/panic attacks, this is now the time to speak to your doc or therapist prescribing them if you would like to discontinue them. Under no circumstances, unless they are an 'as needed' type med, are you to do this on your own.

Confidence, Organization & Focus MP3

Confidence, Organization & Focus is designed to increase these attributes within you, allowing you to smoothly move through your life and world. It allows for a relaxed and focused attitude whether alone or with others, so that in every situation and circumstance in which you find yourself, your self-confidence, self-reliance, self-acceptance and self esteem creates self-sufficiency and optimal results.

Become a stronger individual in a cycle of progress that grows, deepens and reinforces itself every day as you grow and become that individual you have always wanted to be.

☞ Please use this hypnosis session responsibly. Only listen to it where your attentions are not required. Never listen to it while driving. Remember to create about 30 minutes where you are undisturbed, turn off your phone and anything that might distract you. Listen to it all the way through for optimal results. There is no age limit, and is especially helpful for those with ADD, ADHD, Procrastination ideations or issues.

Why do I say procrastination 'ideations'?

Because we often label ourselves in the worst light, that inner critique going on and on like the great OZ behind a curtain.

Many of us perform well under a deadline, the last moment... our focus rallies and intensifies when we perceive we have something to loose or gain. Some people under pressure either fold or focus, which are you?

Procrastination is an important subject. It is the gateway to depression. Why? Because if you continually label yourself as a procrastinator, you are always in the process of failing. Most people do not have a positive opinion of procrastination. So, we are working from that point of view.

☞ Procrastination brings up should, should-ing on ourselves. This is a messy thing.

☞ Procrastination and self trust are intimately intertwined.

When you hold a negative attitude on procrastination, and perhaps fail to see how you primarily operate, you in essence bully yourself, castigate, cajole, curse at you. You say things to yourself that if any other person said to you, especially if your care for or love that person, would hurt you deeply... that self talk.

☞ There is only one way to re-build self trust: Follow through.

If you see the garbage needs to be taken out you can either state to yourself: I will take it out now, or on my way out in the morning. If you discover that you forgot to take out the garbage upon returning home, put down your bags, without comment internally, and tie it up and take it out. Make decisions and then follow through, no matter how mundane or important, make a decision and don't look back. Resentment, criticism and guilt are damaging patterns of stuckness.

☞ How to know if procrastination is negatively affecting your life: You loose friends because you are chronically a no show or late. You loose jobs because you show up late and/or leave early, don't complete your tasks or turn in inferior work.

☞ Imagine this scenario:

An old friend you haven't seen in a while calls you up and says; "Hey, it's been too long since we've seen each other, why don't we meet 5pm Friday at our favorite restaurant for happy hour." You are delighted and agree, looking forward to Friday.

You show up at 5pm, and wait. Your friend is a no show, and hasn't called. You attempt to contact, nothing, you are worried.

Eventually, a day or so later, you connect. Your friend apologizes profusely, being called into an after hours meeting, and just forgot, going home. Yeah, it could happen you're thinking.

"Look", you're friend says, "let me make it up to you, let's meet at that restaurant next Friday, same time, 5pm and I will buy the drinks." A bit put off, but understanding, you agree. Looking forward to Friday. You again show up at 5pm, your friend no where in sight. Perhaps waiting an hour, calling once. No response.

You leave. Eventually you connect to your friend, and the apologies spill.

The baby sitter could not stay or make it. Perfectly plausible. Shit happens. Another profuse apology, your friend saying this time; "Not only will I get happy hour, 'm buying dinner... get the lobster."

Giving the benefit of the doubt, even though instincts throw up red flags... Sigh.

Okay, you agree. so, the days now pass. You wonder, should I call and re-establish our meeting... Then a place opens up and chirps; shit, they are an adult, know better.

You do not trust they will show up. Doubt enters... off setting trust. (familiarity, comfort, center)

The bonds of trust have now been broken. If you ever speak to your friend again, it will take no less than 9 months of consistent follow through behavior before trust is reestablished. And there may remain a question about their integrity or your importance to them for a long time.

We have a relationship with our selves just like with the people in our lives. There is no difference, except with the intensity of personal betrayal or anger you feel when you are disappointed with you. We can walk away from relationships. We cannot walk away from ourselves, except through a type of abandonment through depression, lack of self worth and self esteem, second guessing every decision, a life unbalanced and up in the air. This creates insecurity and does not allow for contentment, comfort, balance, confidence, self acceptance.

There is a difference between confidence and arrogance.

Give yourself permission to move forward Only you can. As you build a stronger inner personal relationship with you, you will live in your dynamic center, from your authentic self.

Earlier I mentioned that you are the creator and co-creator in your life. We are not consciously aware of everything going on in and around our lives. This is where trust also enters, trust in yourself and timing. There Is a timing to things, so don't push the river, flow with it. You have a rudder to steer by. Trust in delays, they may be a blessing unrecognized.

Self Trust & Serenity MP3

It is not somewhere along our lives we lost trust in ourselves. It occurs over time. When we were children we trusted without question, ourselves. As time moved on, we may have received messages not to trust self, by parents or teachers and especially our peers.

There are many reason too numerous to list here how you forgot to trust yourself. As you have learned, you are the thinker and decider in your own mind. To second guess yourself or out n out not trust yourself is akin to denying Divine Source, or there is another better suited to make decisions in your life beyond you. You have to live with the consequences of the choices you make, no other.

When you trust yourself, and more so, trust your intuition, you are the master of your life, of your domain, and ultimately of your experiences along life.

Mis-takes are a part of the process of growth, of evolution of the self. Accept and embrace all of your flaws, faults, insufficiencies, foibles... it is par for the course.

You are one of a kind, there has never been anyone like you, nor will there be. You are unique. And, more importantly, you are required. If you weren't, you would not be here. Trust ME on this point, until you realize this.

Anxiety & Panic Relief MP3

If after the second use of the Mind-Spa session you are still experiencing symptoms, use this MP3. Gain control of Anxiety and Panic Attacks. For optimal results, please use headphones. This recording is 26:22 minutes in length. Learn how to relax and release bodily tension. Learn how to control your breath and shut down the rush of adrenaline (Fight or Flight or Freeze Response) Learn to eliminate a panic attack in less than three minutes. Learn to correct permanently, anxiety and panic attacks.

☞ You will only use this recording in a safe place, NEVER while driving or as background or subliminally. * Tips: To leach the adrenaline from your body, sip room temperature water, takes about 7 minutes. To relax your stomach and discomfort drink Mint tea, take a mint, such as Altoids. An Apple also works for calming the stomach and stimulating appetite. Do the Reset Button Technique 3-5 times.

To release tension, relax your jaw, drop your shoulders and relax your belly. Now take in a deep breath, pause for a second or two, then exhale, blowing the air out of your mouth like you are blowing soap bubbles... do this very slowly. Continue 5- 10 times, paying attention to your shoulders remaining in a relaxed position I call this the "Reset Button" exercise. To stop rapid thoughts, Stop thinking about the future, all anxiety is based on your thoughts of the future. Anchor yourself in the Present moment. Change your location, take a walk, write an email, etc. Get out of your head and into your environment.

Did You Know...

Thought

Emotion   Feeling

Emotion Thought Feeling

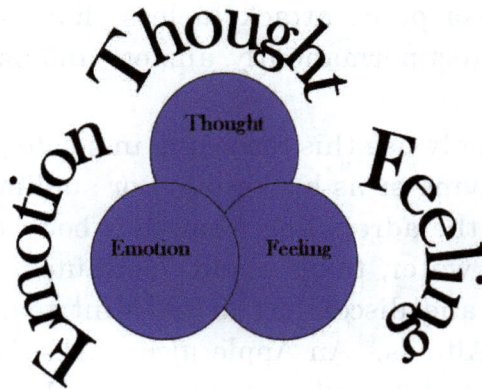

A Message of
Choice & Change

By Kate A. Ellis,CCHt

Did You Know...
A Message of Choice & Change Book

Here are reviews that beautifully speaks to the content:

When I started reading "Did You Know," I immediately thought of Eckhart Tolle and "Power of Now" and how much better Kate Ellis' little book is, especially in a practical way.

Mind you, this is just after reading a page.

How did I know? Mostly because I know Kate Ellis fairly well and I took a bit of time to investigate Mr. Tolle when I first looked at his work.

It is my habit to study the author's background and motivations to evaluate better what I am reading, especially when the material is presumed to be important for a person's life.

And what is more important than a person's life? Not the author's life so much, but your life as reader, which the author's work is supposed to help enhance. I believe that reading is not just about having some awareness, but more about getting real results.

The image that comes to mind in comparing "Did You Know" with "Power of Now" is that of swimming in deep waters versus stepping through a shallow pond. As you can imagine they are very different experiences and each has its own value and reward.

It appears that Tolle wrote and worked his book to become a popular spiritual author. He succeeded in that.

When it comes to Kate's little book, it seems that she wrote it for herself as much as for anybody else. She didn't tell me this; I am inferring, and of course I may be wrong. What I know about Kate is that she is a serious person who at times will do the work and always strives to do her best for her clients.

What I come away with in reading "Did You Know" is Kate's own struggles in thinking hard about the connections among thoughts, emotions and feelings and how they affect our lives. She is presenting us with her findings at the point in time that she was writing.

Because Kate can think deeply, "Did You Know" offers considerable value... if you are willing to do the work, learn about yourself and extract the value. The book is brief. There are many pages with one or two ideas, and others with a set of words and phrases. I want to emphasize that because it is why this book can be more valuable for you.

This is a book that you need to carry around with a notebook (paper or electronic), and then you read and re-read and write (or dictate.) You will get a lot of value, not because you agree with the material, but because you use it as a foil to arrive at your own conclusions.

For me, that is why Kate's "Did You Know" has more practical importance than most best-selling books relating to self-growth and personal development.

Jim Namaste,Ph.D.

"Did You Know" by Kate Ellis provides a simple pathway of learning about how the thought/feeling/emotion/belief processes of our minds work. She gently guides the reader with educational steps on how to take charge of our mind - the reward being a more peaceful and balanced state of being. She concludes her guide with fun techniques on maintaining a focused, quiet space that strengthens our ability to clearly focus and relax our mind in the present. A delightful read with wisdom for everyone!

Triza Schultz, author of the book, "The Fear Standard - A Guide And Personal Journey To Regain Our Intuitive Spirit"

Kate has beautifully and poetically composed the simple truths of self-mastery. Artistically written, Kate has created a readable hypnotic journey sure to transform how you think...therefore how you feel. I highly recommend "Did You Know?" to be your constant pocket or purse companion....certain to be your loving reminder of your perpetual creatorship.

Michelle Lee, CH Founder of Athena Rising Now a program dedicated to freeing teens girls, their mothers, and all women from ancient cultural programming to become the leaders they were born to be.
www.AthenaRisingNow.com

Kate Ellis is able to convey a plethora of wisdoms that have been passed down through the centuries.

Kate's style is rather poetic, and like most good poetry it instills thought.... sometimes deep thoughts..

You stand to be commended, and I would definitely recommend this read to anyone.

Rod Kelly, BCH. Board Certified Consulting Hypnotist

Enough-ism, BLAZE A UNIQUE TRAIL

WORDS THAT EMPOWER

SECRET MIND TRANSFORMATION TO INCREASE
INTENTION, INTUITION AND CONSCIOUSNESS
"YOU ARE AN UNENDING HORIZON"

by Kate Ellis

Words That Empower Play Books

We are continually 'empowering' or 'disempowering' ourselves by what we think or say. Language is the extension of your current belief system and your attitudes.

Do you have challenges meditating? The few minutes playing the affirmation solves that!

Most of us do not know how to properly word an affirmation that will have a potent effect to change your perception and life. Have you tried before without any effective changes?

It takes 88-1000 times repeating an affirmation before it begins to manifest in your life. Each puzzle length is designed to enhance new connections in your subconscious and in your brain.

Everything required that makes affirmations work, the thoughts and attitude needed to change your life is all within the intention of these innovative affirmation puzzles.

☞ Overcome your limiting beliefs

☞ Release fear of change.

☞ We all gravitate towards what is comfortable or what is familiar. Change can only occur through expanding your boundaries.

☞ Re-wire your brain to conquer depression, anxiety, procrastination.

You are a body, mind and spirit, a soul in chemical clothing. Positive thoughts release endorphins, and pleasure chemicals.

Words that Empower *word search puzzles* are especially crafted to shift your attention and focus your intention through a fun word-search format. These puzzles utilizes subtle forms of neural linguistic programming, (NLP) affirmations (saying 'yes' to yourself) and visualization (imagery, using your five senses) techniques to reprogram your consciousness in ways you previously thought not possible.

LANGUAGE & Imagination programs our subconscious which directs us to successfully achieve our desires or if used negatively to possibly limit our goals. Words are powerful tools, and used properly will enhance self-esteem and sets you up on a course for success in every area of your life. You are an unending horizon of potentiality. If you are familiar with the philosophies and teachings of Louise Hay, Deepak Chopra, Tony Robbins and other wonderful authors of this genre, you will enjoy these easy yet challenging word search puzzles and identify in a playful way how to maximize your success and desires. These word search puzzles guide you through a series of positive goals and games to enhance ones life.

Words that Empower effectiveness primarily lies on the placement of the word-lines within the puzzle-box. The psychology of the collection of words is intentionally placed in various areas of the puzzle subliminally effect the subconscious and is quite stimulating. As one reads the word combinations it becomes an affirmation. You begin to focus your attention on positive empowering words and concepts. The affirmations grow and strengthens as the puzzle is being completed. Some puzzles are in alphabetical order and others are designed as a mantra one could repeat to oneself. Both have a programming effect on the brain and the subconscious, while relaxing with a game.

Who benefits from

Words That Empower

"Enough-ism, blaze a unique trail" vol IV

☞ Anyone wanting to reduce stress & strengthen focus

Adolescents and young adults who are beginning to form life's belief patterns and attitudes

Balance and harmonize the mind-body-spirit

Eliminate worn out negative patterns and re-program positive life supporting ones

Elderly and anyone who wants to strengthen mind alertness

Enhance and strengthen cognitive abilities

Enjoys games & entertainment with a purpose

Enjoys a progressive mental challenge

Reinforce knowledge & affirmations

As a meditation practice

A way to play without guilt

Absorbs time and Enriches the mind

Focuses on self improvement

The Healing Quest Audio
Hypnotherapy Programs

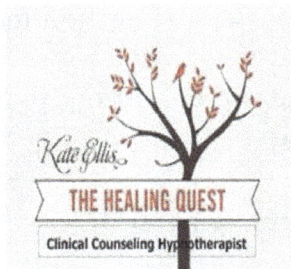

**Magic 21 Ultimate Lifestyle,
Weight Maintenance,
Anxiety Elimination & Depression
Release MP3
Hypnosis & Counseling Program**

Magic 21 Special Offer

If You Are Struggling With:

- Weight or Body Image Issues;
- Anxieties; Inner, Social, Self-Esteem;
- Depression, Life Is Too Hard...

Highlights of Magic 21:

Your program runs approximately the course of six months with
personal attention to your journey including access to professional counseling
along your journey through;
Phone, Email, and/or Skype Sessions.

**Magic 21 is an nightly hypnosis program designed to
allow permanent shifts and transition into a new level of your best self,
physically, emotionally and spiritually,
all while you are sleeping.**

**For interview please email: kellis19@hotmail.com
Please include your phone # with best times to consult.**

Exclusive offer participation is limited.

Does life feel like you are going around in circles - lost in the noise?

Magic 21 Nightly Hypnosis MP3 & Counseling Program can help you break this cycle. See results within 2-4 weeks! Many even sooner, like the next morning.

Magic 21 name derives from the 21 Hypnosis MP3's you will receive every 7-14 days.

What is the significance of the # 21? When you seek to create lasting changes in your life, it take 21 days of focus before the old pattern is dislodged and changes can Now begin.

During this 6 month journey together, you will continue to progress and delight in releasing whatever is internally inhibiting you, and embrace all that allows you to experience your every potential.

Throughout your journey you have access to Kate Ellis,ccht for phone, skype, text, email consultations & counseling. Assisting you through any challenges you may encounter. Never get 'stuck' again in your journey of recover, discovery and brilliance.

Outline of each of the Magic 21 MP3's

1. Mind-Spa Ultimate Healing:

Clears emotional baggage from the conscious and subconscious mind. Removes brain clutter, old tapes/conditioning/programming. Balance brain chemicals & hormones. Relieves procrastination, anxiety (*for those with panic attacks, often resets the fight/flight/freeze response often eliminating panic attacks) depression, low energy, resets circadian rhythm (sleep cycle) improving the quality of sleep. By clearing the mind of unnecessary baggage, it creates a clean slate to in-put lifestyle changes.

2. **Enhanced Flavor of Food**: Weight/Body Image #1

Feel completely satisfied mentally & physically with well balanced meals. Relax desire to snack in between meals and begin shifting eating out of nervousness, tenseness, boredom, frustration, depression or anger. You will begin to naturally gravitate towards healthier food choices.

3. **Addressing & Altering Behavior**: Weight/Body Image #2:

The elements, such as perception, beliefs and time orientation with the aim of these patterns to effect behavioral change in line with desired outcome.

Incorporates flexibility, balance, self protection for those who do not place themselves at center or as a priority, with many obligations such as family, work and who overextend themselves. Aim; activate foresight & better organize daily schedule.

4. **Foresight**:

The goal is to change behavior for many issues to find solutions, emphasizing foresight, patience & flexibility. Embracing these 3 skills, solutions comes to your awareness.

5. **Accessing Well Being**:

Motivates you to greater access to well being, making healthy choices in present & future mentally and physically. Drawing naturally occurring forms of how the subconscious looks out for one's best interest, unconsciously guiding to greater well being.

6. **Moving Forward, Self Support**:

You will access internal resources, reworking some things in life differently, for optimal results.

7. **Behaving Naturally**: This addresses those who try too hard, releasing internal/personality issues of placing too much pressure on self in every area of life, allowing you to express yourself naturally without worrying what others think and relaxing your own self doubts.

8. **Initiating Action**:

Increases awareness of pace in life and managing time. Encouraging looking within at details below the surface to seek a natural pace, neither too fast or too slow. Unpleasant emotional states are identified and relied on to provide energy which can be used to motivate change.

9. **Maintaining Momentum**:

Sustaining change into the future. (1) Maintaining change so it becomes permanent.

(2) Addressing natural concerns of newly implemented lifestyle may fade or vanish.

(3) Continuing to deepen & expand new personal lifestyle.

10. **Action Beyond Planning**:

Addressing tendencies of those who extensively plan without ever moving from the planning stage, especially for perfectionists. Converting raw energy of frustration into actions towards goals.

11. **Behavior Over Time**:

Examine previous choices. We break up old patterns that tend to repeat out of habit. We remove old paths and allow new routes in direction of choice.

12. Modifying Impulses:

We address impulsive tendencies. You will develop pacing yourself from overindulging and alternative responses.

13. Making Change:

We address tendency of holding on to old behavior patterns that have out-lived their usefulness. Addressing resistance & hesitation to let go of old patterns & openness to new ones.

14. Matching Resources To The Situation:

Creating best outcome. We address those who have a tendency to force-fit behavior & need to prove competency & feelings of incompetence & fears of outcome. We create an open mindedness & flexibility that allows better outcomes.

15. Life Long Learning:

Identify steps in learning and the cues that allow you to combine new and old lessons. Promotes faster learning, trusting self & others.

16. Breaking A Habit:

Habits that involve unnecessary resources or actions; Positive emotions are tied to new behaviors that changes patterns.

17. Becoming Self Directed:

Taking initiative in spite of others and their attempt to influence. Overcome autocratic treatment of self. Focus on self directed behavior.

18. **Weight/Body Image** #3:

Leaving past ways behind. Fine tuning new ones of lifestyle and accessing states & behavior that bring positive change.

19. **Day Begins Before You Awaken**:

Creating a different perspective in the present, permitting more flexibility in thinking & breaking old habits and replacing them with new more effective ways of behaving.

20. **Roots Of Choice**:

Aims at early stages of decision making process. Better understand ingredients that precede decisions. Recruit more useful resources that will enhance effectiveness of decisions, developing deeper insight and increase foresight of greater clarity about self, options and goals.

21. **Releasing The Past**:

Helps release you from ruminating about the past, letting go of past and extract beneficial content so you can move on into the present and future more effectively.

> **"I am not what happened to me, I am what I choose to become."**
>
> —Carl Gustav Jung

What people are saying about Magic 21

I listened to audio 1 on July 1st and right away relaxed for a very restful night sleep. Day after things seemed different in the way I could see and feel. I didn't feel so attached to everything. Felt more like an observer. I wasn't as irritated with the noises or things that had annoyed me before.

Food: am not experiencing any cravings. Feeling full. Not even interested in anything sweet. Had been experiencing digestive issues, not feeling as gassy or sleepy. I feel more hopeful.

My responses to others are more on point. It's easier to say what I feel as if I have more self-worth suddenly. Don't feel as subject to others opinions or need for their permission. Feeling more empowered in my work and getting things done on my own instead of feeling so needy for help.

Sleeping 7 to 8 hours each night. I made a new ritual starting at same time as this program to set my alarm when I go to bed for 7.5-8 hours of sleep. Just getting 30-60 more minutes each night I feel better. Feel like the hypnosis is adding to the relaxation too. Dv

Two days after the last audio I was having a low energy day but needed to go to Costco to get groceries. I just left no makeup, in my yoga pants and t-shirt and flip flops...felt kinda embarrassed because I usually don't go out like that. But it was weird. As I walked through the store it was really surreal. Everyone was smiling at me, including other shoppers. Then it was like there were several men who were around every corner. Then in the checkout line the guy behind me was talking to me about my avocadoes and everyone processing me out was out of the ordinary friendly. Usually when you go to that store there's so many people rushing about and stressing...the experience really stood out to me as out of the ordinary.

Other experiences with people feels like there's less between us, like people are more present with me. Being present is something that I have done a lot of work in and notice when people are not so present, so it's felt good.

Feeling more relaxed in life, not as stressed.
Looking forward to the next session. dv

🖋   I am doing well. Eating more protein and vegetables. I am being as active as my knees will let me. Pain, does slow me down. I feel very strong and anxiety free. Many projects getting done. Not putting things off any more. Very happy.. Rs

🖋   I have had no desire to use eye blinders to sleep since first tape. I have used them to sleep for 12 years. A wonderful side affect. Have had no chocolate since 2nd tape. Buying and eating healthier. More re energy. Getting projects done I been putting off. Thank you for this program and benefits I am deceiving. Blessings, Ro

🖋   I've noticed quite a few things, esp this past week. First, with the second program, I tend to " go under" much more quickly than the first. I find a floating feeling while my body feels as though I

don't care to move it, I'm so blissfully relaxed. Also, I have not been able to make it through the second one awake one time. I know you said this doesn't matter, so I'm not concerned.

I am not waking up in pain everyday as I used to. Taking a pain pill with coffee used to be my normal breakfast. Now I sometimes don't need one for several hours. My appetite is greatly decreased, I'm, at times, needing to take the time to make a meal to ensure I'm eating properly. I'm walking to the store instead of driving, the other day I opted to walk home from the baseball game instead of having my son drive me home.

Anxiety I had with work has greatly decreased. I had just started buspar prior to this program, but I'm hoping to be able to wean off of that then start looking at decreasing my Prozac with my doctor. I'll see her in 2 weeks. I have not had to take any xanax. My sleep is fantastic, even with all the added work stress I've had. I'm a true believer in this!! I feel so much lighter, happier when I wake up, more positive. Thank you. Ds

🖋 Weight loss journey. my friend Angie said if you leave food on your plate you will never be fat. my weight today was 212. last night i listened to the first mp3 made by kate ellis. at **11:00** am, i opened the refrigerator and my mind started talking to me about cheese. do you need the cheese on your egg. oh, course. oh not really. "do you need the cheese on the egg". my mind asked me, " do you need the cheese on the egg" at least four times. i did not put cheese on the egg was a final decision. i put cholula on the egg and i did not miss the cheese! HA HA vs

🖋 I had a dream last night......more perhaps like a revelation or hopefully a light upon my deep feelings of low self esteem/ inadequacy/fear. I saw myself as a boy sitting with a man. I'm not sure if it was my father. I think this man actually had lighter hair (my Dad had dark hair).

What i do know is that whatever was said, it explains everything. It was either this man telling me I was useless, or him telling me about someone else telling me that I am. I remember trying to wake up so I could remember exactly what happened. It might have also been me sitting with someone whom I felt I could never be like - happy/successful etc. t was brief yet obviously powerful. sb

🖋 I listened to session 2 last night and as with the other, fell asleep quickly. Slept well and have been a little more focused/calm since Tuesday.

Sb

"Echoes of Ancient Wounds"
Healing the Inner Child
Nightly Hypnosis & Counseling MP3 Program

Each Hypnosis MP3 program leads deeper into healing unresolved issues emanating from childhood. Wounds you may not even remember on a conscious level that continues patterns of behavior that feel as though you are stuck. Often we have ingrained foundational belief systems that constantly tell you things like; you are wrong, you are not good enough, you do not deserve love, success or happiness.

These deep inner feelings began when you were little. Children need parents/guardians for love, support, nurturing, shelter, food, drink and above all safe & protected. We become negatively imprinted when these needs are unfulfilled or if a parent/guardian imposed a type of reward system, such as giving you attention or love when they approve of you or what you did, such as bringing home good grades, or doing your chores correctly, etc. A part of us becomes deeply insecure, and as an adult seeks the approval of others. Many of our relationships can be abusive, where you put up with bad behavior, yelling, degrading you. This is what you experienced as a child, and feels normal to you though none the less hurts. You become trapped in bad relationships and do not know why.

This audio is designed to be used either during the day or to go to sleep to. The advantage of going to bed listening, you may allow it to loop all night. Your mind will marinate and absorb only the information it needs to align your mind, body and yes spirit towards creating your life as an artist might, becoming inspired at just the right time & uninhibited. Have you experienced that flow before, where one thing flows into the next effortlessly, easily... Some call it the zone. Michael Angelo once said; the statue is already in the stone, I simply remove the excess material...

This series, echoes of ancient wounds is designed to liberate you from imprints from the past, from childhood and traumas growing up. Really any trauma that hinders your ability to move forward, with only your voice in your head, not echoes of parents or teachers, friends or other family members that may have left a negative impression, or imprint.

Sometimes we don't even realize what is holding us back, why we may hesitate or lack confidence, have bouts of depression or anxiety that seem to make no sense.

Often we have belief's that are out moded, meaning; they do not reflect who we are in the present day. Perhaps when you were younger you were told you were not smart or attractive or capable in some way, shape or form. A part of you then absorbed this information and took it as a truth. It may have been at some point, but not now. You have grown and evolved so much since then, yet sometimes we fail to recognize that and still inside react like a vulnerable little child, believing without question what we are told.

You are now on a journey to update your foundational belief systems, and reveal your authentic self that has been covered by debris all along. The you you really are, and not the judgments of others or your decisions henceforth. Remember, you are an unending horizon, and the only limits you have are the ones you accept.

So, get comfy, prepare to relax and heal your inner child and change the dynamic & paradigm of your life allowing you to move forward comfortably, confidently and boldly, you are life unbounded. You are the master of your mind, you are the ruler of your body. KAE

A brief description of each of the programs

1. "Smoky the Bear," Dealing with abdominal, digestive and elimination issues. There is a mind-body connection via your emotional being. Often physiological issues resolved and even sometime unresolved manifest as diseases & disorders.

2. Tension producing emotional states can manifest as irritability, depression, effect appetite, create anxiety and frustration. This session works on easing both emotional and physiological disturbances.

3. Walking in Comfort is designed to shift you from an anxiety reaction in a particular situation to a relaxed, calm response to the same situation.

4. Stress Response is designed to mitigate overreacting to minor stress or challenges. It helps you consciously and subconsciously chose an alternative response to usual overreaction expecting the worst. Sometimes reactions are reacting from a negative emotional state, to eating unhealthy foods, some people even break out in rashes.

5. Limiting beliefs formed in childhood, Often the childhood beliefs in the midst of trauma are the ones we revert to and do not update. These beliefs stem from very limited cognitive abilities we possess during our childhood. This session begins the updating process from unresolved issues and limiting belief systems.   (27:31)

6. Our inner self, our healthy, natural self, allows for more effective orientation in time and accessing of healthy resources.

7. Garden of your life is designed to release negative self talk, especially those well rooted in a faulty past belief system. We essentially burn these self defeating ideas, beliefs and inner self talk and plant new seeds of optimism.

8. Recovering from past wounds addresses releasing and healing past wounds in order to develop new personal growth in the future This is especially effective for people who often feel stuck.

9. Accessing resource states addresses the conscious, unconscious and potentially deeper levels of the unconscious. Personal conflict can stem from a battle of control between the conscious and unconscious mind. This session seeks to release emotional injuries and their debris that interfere with retrieving the resource residing in our deeper psyche.

10. Choosing states with foresight aims to utilize past learning and emotional states to increase foresight and awareness of choice for both the present and the future. Continuing to release emotional baggage.

11. Grief relief addresses a process often called regret. This is for those who regret event or events in the past that we wish unfolded differently which often leads to a state of chronic frustration. Regret involves focusing on specifics of the past, the details. But the present and the future hold general opportunities to achieve what you want to happen... now.

kae

Recommended Books

You Can Heal Your Life By Louise Hay

Holographic Universe By Michael Talbot

Remember your Essence By Paul Williams

The Nature of Personal Reality By Jane Roberts

Illusions, Adventures of a reluctant Messiah By Richard Bach

Jonathan Livingston Segal By Richard Bach

Callings, Finding and Following an Authentic Life By Gregg LeVoy

The Tao of Synchronicity By Jean Shinoda Bolen

The Hero with a Thousand Faces By Joseph Campbell

Fire in the Soul or Anything by Joan Borysenko

Creative Visualization By Shakti Gawain

The Urban Shaman By Serge King

Way of the Peaceful Warrior By Dan Millman

Results Not Typical By Dr Lewis Heller

Mythic Tarot By Juliet Sharman-Burke & Liz Greene

(serves as an excellent way to understand our journey through life via the Greek myths)

Any Nature Guide of your immediate area

Women, From Profit to Power, Your Guide to Claiming Your Worth By Michelle Lee

Anatomy of the Spirit By Caroline Myss

The Untethered Soul By Michael Singer

Tao Te Ching

The Tao of Physics By Frank Capra

The Art of War By Sun Tzu

(Remember) Be Here Now By Ram Dass

Women Who Run With The Wolves By Clarissa Pinkola Estes

Hands of Light By Barbara Ann Brennan

Michael's Gemstone Dictionary

Psychological Types By CG Jung

Memories, Dreams, Reflections By CG Jung

Many Lives, Many Masters By Brian Weiss

The Missing Piece By Shel Silverstein

Parabola Magazine

Ions/Noetic Science Magazine

The Elegant Universe By Brian Greene

The Hero and the Goddess By Jean Houston

Anything By Edgar Casey

The Biology of Belief By Dr Bruce Lipton

Journey of the Soul By Dr Michael Newton

I consider this last book a book that needs to be in every home:

Life 101, You can't afford the luxury of a negative thought

By John Rogers & Peter McWilliams

Any Life 101 Series

Journey Of Souls By Dr Michael Newton

Destiny Of Souls By Dr Michael Newton

Wisdom Of Souls By Newton Institute

Credit where credit is due

Some graphics (public domain) were gathered online, through Google searches and Facebook friends, as well as along the years long forgotten. Thank you Public Domain.

Page 34: Inspiring and Positive Quotes; Facebook

Page 37: Jenny Harper LeBel; Facebook

Page 40: Lao Tzu; Facebook

Page 42: Barbara M Moreau & Frank Austin

Page 45: Google

Page 65: Scott Sonnon; Facebook

Page 88: Barbara Moreau and Frank J. Austin

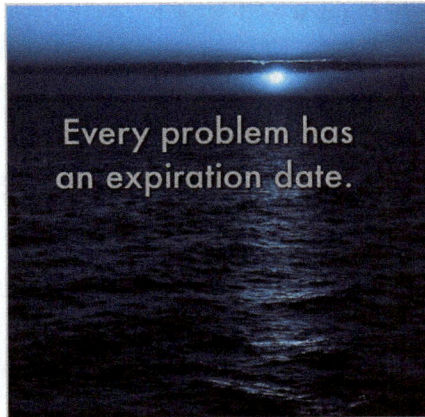

Every problem has an expiration date.

Kate Ellis, CCHt. is a Clinical Counseling Hypnotherapist for over 30 years specializing in the relief and remission of anxiety and panic attacks and teaches techniques for optimum living. She is a consultant and teacher exploring psychological growth, healing, intuition, creativity, hypnosis and spirituality. Kate has a private practice, The Healing Quest, in Scottsdale, Arizona.

Kate served as the Vice President (2013-2015) & President (2016-2017) now, Emeritus for the Arizona Society For Professional Hypnosis, Founded in 1978 ASPH is Arizona's only independent professional Hypnosis & Hypnotherapy organization. It is one of the largest active Hypnosis & Hypnotherapy membership groups in the country.

ASPH www.hypnosisaz.com

Contact Kate via email @

kellis19@hotmail.com

www.thehealingquest.com

Facebook.com/thehealingquest

Facebook.com/mindful.puzzles

SOMETIMES
THE SMALLEST STEP
IN THE RIGHT DIRECTION
ENDS UP BEING THE BIGGEST
STEP OF YOUR LIFE.
TIP TOE IF YOU MUST,
BUT TAKE
THE STEP.

Words that Empower is a continuing affirmation & meditation word search puzzle series.

Additional Titles can be ordered directly from the Author,

www.thehealingquest.com or email; kellis19@hotmail.com

Scottsdale, Arizona

Puzzles:

Words that Empower Volume I, "The Word" (pub. 1997) (Out of print)

Words that Empower Volume II, "Essentials" (pub1998) (Reprint 2009)

Words that Empower Volume III, "Prosperity and Wealth" (pub. 2007) (Reprint 2009)

Words that Empower Volume IV, "GRACES" (pub. 2009)

Words that Empower Volume V, "The sayings of the Buddha" (pub 2010)

Words that Empower Volume VI "Enough-ism, blaze a unique trail" (pub. 2011)

Words that Empower Volume VII "Your Callings" (pub. 2011)

Words that Empower Volume VIII "Honor, Value & Integrity" (pub. 2012)

Words that Empower Volume IX "Contemplations" (pub 2017)

Mindgames /Words that Empower Copyright 1997

By Kate Ellis,ccht

Non-Fiction:

Did You Know...A Message of Choice & Change, (pub. 2006)

An aging master grew tired of his apprentice's complaints. One morning, he sent him to get some salt. When the apprentice returned, the master told him to mix a handful of salt in a glass of water and then drink it.

"How does it taste?" the master asked. "Bitter," said the apprentice.

The master chuckled and then asked the young man to take the same handful of salt and put it in the lake. The two walked in silence to the nearby lake and once the apprentice swirled his handful of salt in the water, the old man said, "Now drink from the lake."

As the water dripped down the young man's chin, the master asked, "How does it taste?" "Fresh," remarked the apprentice. "Do you taste the salt?" asked the master.
"No," said the young man.
At this the master sat beside this serious young man, and explained softly,

"The pain of life is pure salt; no more, no less. The amount of pain in life remains exactly the same. However, the amount of bitterness we taste depends on the container we put the pain in. So when you are in pain, the only thing you can do is to enlarge your sense of things. Stop being a glass. Become a lake."

www.ingramcontent.com/pod-product-compliance
Lightning Source LLC
Chambersburg PA
CBHW060259100426
42742CB00011B/1812